"When I received my first Bible, the King James Version was recognized as the standard translation of Scripture. Things have changed considerably during my lifetime. Developments in Bible translation theories and the proliferation of versions and paraphrases necessitate that those committed to the authoritative Word of God carefully compare and contrast translation theories. Leland Ryken's passionate defense of essentially literal translations and his polemic against dynamic equivalence is one readers of the English Bible should carefully consider. Ryken persuaded me that, as a pastor, this is an area I must monitor more carefully."

—Chris Brauns, author, *Unpacking Forgiveness*; Pastor, The Red Brick Church, Stillman Valley, Illinois

"When it comes to the Word of God, I feel very childlike, almost naïve. I believe the Bible is what is says it is—words breathed out by God. Consequently I need to live by every word that comes from his mouth. So why would this book hold a valued place in my library? Because it affirms to me the absolute necessity of translations that not only respect each inspired word but also trust that our omniscient, omnipotent God is able by his Spirit to help his people understand what it means. Through his scholarship Ryken's work affirms to me what I know by faith: that if I am to truly honor God as God, I must have and study a Bible translated by scholars who not only tremble at his every 'purified' word (Ps. 12:6) but also do not assume they know better than God how to speak to his people today. Ryken gives me the facts, the fuel, and the fire I need to continue to charge others to use a Bible translation that honors God by hanging on his every word. God has spoken. God can make it understood. We simply need to be faithful to handle it accurately. As his slave, I am to serve him, not help him! I do not think I could say with the psalmist, 'For you, yourself have taught me' (119:102), if I didn't use a Bible that honors God's word and his style and will not violate it, and consequently him, by playing God in an attempt to translate for the reader."

—Kay Arthur, Co-CEO, Precept Ministries International

"This is an important book for anyone who reads the Bible in English. Ryken clarifies recent dramatic evolutions in translation theory, offering a distinct contrast between the centuries-old stream of essentially literal translation and the decades-old stream of dynamic equivalency. Ryken does not ignore nuances, but with clarity and wit he offers every person the chance and the responsibility to grasp the issues at stake at a crucial time in the history of these issues. Not only does Ryken urge respect for the biblical text, with its original words intended by the authors and inspired by God the author; he also encourages respect for the Bible's readers, who deserve the privilege of reading and studying this God-given text, loving and penetrating its literary beauty, and being enlarged by words and worlds outside of their own knowledge and experience. Ryken helpfully debunks many current myths—like the one that mistakes essentially literal translation for transliteration or the one that claims all translation is essentially interpretation. Most of all, Ryken's call to is to guard and treasure a stable biblical text, which has for centuries clearly spoken God's truth into his world, so that we will hear no our own voices but God's."

—Kathleen B. Nielson, author and speaker


"Leland Ryken, in this scholarly yet understandable volume, exposes the dynamic equivalence theory of Bible translation as not only insufficient but counterproductive in that it of necessity moves its practitioners from being translators of the Bible to interpreters, commentators, and even editors of the Bible. In staking out a return to literal equivalence, he not only reclaims the translator's priority commitment of faithfulness to the divine Author's words but simultaneously affirms a high view of Scripture and an invigorating encouragement to Bible study as well as expositional preaching."

—Harry L. Reeder III, Minister of Preaching and Leadership,
Briarwood Presbyterian Church, Birmingham, Alabama

# Understanding
## English
## Bible Translation

Crossway titles by Leland Ryken:

*ESV Literary Study Bible*
*The Word of God in English: Criteria for Excellence in Bible Translation*
*Choosing a Bible: Understanding Bible Translation Differences*
*Preach the Word: Essays on Expository Preaching: In Honor of R. Kent Hughes (co-editor)*

# Understanding
# English
# Bible Translation

## THE CASE FOR AN ESSENTIALLY LITERAL APPROACH

## LELAND RYKEN

**∷ CROSSWAY** WHEATON, ILLINOIS

Interior design and typesetting: Lakeside Design Plus
Cover design: Studio Gearbox
First printing 2009
Printed in the United States of America

All emphases in Scripture references have been added by the author.

Trade paperback ISBN:  978-1-4335-0279-8
PDF ISBN:              978-1-4335-1261-2
Mobipocket ISBN:     978-1-4335-1262-9

**Library of Congress Cataloging-in-Publication Data**
Ryken, Leland.
    Understanding English Bible translation : the case for an essentially literal approach / Leland Ryken.
      p. cm.
    Includes index.
    ISBN 978-1-4335-0279-8 (tpb)
    1. Bible—Translating. 2. Bible. English. 3. Bible—Criticism, interpretation, etc.
    I. Title.

BS449.R949 2009
220.5'2001—dc22

                                           2009007850

| VP | | 20 | 19 | 18 | 17 | 16 | 15 | 14 | 13 | 12 | 11 | 10 | 09 |
|----|----|----|----|----|----|----|----|----|----|----|----|----|----|
| 14 | 13 | 12 | 11 | 10 | 9 | 8 | 7 | 6 | 5 | 4 | 3 | 2 | 1 |

For Kent and Barbara Hughes

# CONTENTS

Preface                                                          13

Part One: Overview of Issues                                     15

1. Understanding English Bible Translation                       17
2. Questions and Answers about English Bible
   Translation                                                   23

Part Two: The Story of English Bible Translation                35

3. Laying the Foundation                                         37
4. Building on the Foundation                                    47
5. Building on Another Foundation                                57

Part Three: The Two Main Genres of Modern
   English Bible Translation                                     67

6. Divergent Goals for Bible Translation                         69
7. Divergent Views of the Bible                                  79
8. Divergent Views of the Bible's Authors, Readers,
   and Translators                                               89
9. Divergent Methods of Translation                              99
10. Divergent Styles of Translation                              107

**Part Four: The Ideal English Bible Translation**          119

11. Fullness Rather Than Reductionism                        121
12. Transparency to the Original Text                        131
13. Preserving the Literary Qualities of the Bible           139

**Part Five: The Bible in the Church**                       151

14. Oral Reading of the Bible                                153
15. The Need for a Translation That People Can Trust
    and Respect                                              163
16. Teaching and Preaching from the Bible                    173

Appendix A: Statements from Preachers
            and Bible Study Experts                          183
Appendix B: Ten Reasons You Can Trust an
            Essentially Literal Bible Translation            189

Notes                                                        195
Index                                                        201
Permissions                                                  207

# ABBREVIATIONS OF BIBLE

# TRANSLATIONS

| | |
|---|---|
| AMP | Amplified Bible |
| CEV | Contemporary English Version |
| ESV | English Standard Version |
| GNB | Good News Bible |
| HCSB | Holman Christian Standard Bible |
| JB | Jerusalem Bible |
| KJV | King James Version |
| MESSAGE | The Message |
| NASB | New American Standard Version |
| NCV | New Century Version |
| NEB | New English Bible |
| NIV | New International Version |
| NIVI | New International Version Inclusive Language Edition |
| NKJV | New King James Version |
| NLT | New Living Translation |
| NLV | New Life Version |
| NRSV | New Revised Standard Version |
| PHILLIPS | New Testament in Modern English |

| | |
|---|---|
| REB | Revised English Bible |
| RSV | Revised Standard Verison |
| SEB | Simple English Bible |
| TLB | The Living Bible |
| TNIV | Today's New International Version |

# PREFACE

THIS IS A BOOK about the theory and practice of English Bible translation. Its aim is to clarify the current English Bible translation scene and to present arguments in favor of an essentially literal translation philosophy as being better than dynamic equivalence.

From the very beginning, English Bible translation has existed within definite cultural situations. The current context is one of controversy and debate to a degree that did not characterize earlier eras of Bible translation. Both sides of the current debate have evolved arguments in favor of their positions and counterarguments against criticism of them. Regardless of what side a person takes, much is to be gained by having the arguments laid out to view. I hope that my book will clarify the issues, even for readers who do not agree with my viewpoint.

One of the good effects of the current debate is that Bible readers are more aware of the issues of Bible translation than they were a decade ago. Before a backlash arose against dynamic equivalence, most people who read the NIV or NLT, for example, did not have a clue as to what they were holding in their hands. Today many of these readers do know what they are holding.

Furthermore, anyone who reads the blogs dealing with Bible translation issues cannot help but be struck by how often the word *literal* appears. This is one evidence among several that the tide of unquestioned acceptance of dynamic equivalence is ebbing. My earlier book on Bible translation, *The Word of God in English*,[1] was a comprehensive exploration of the whole field. My current book argues for the same translation philosophy and practice that my earlier book did, but it does so within the altered landscape that now exists.

This is a shorter, more streamlined book than my earlier book. In the interests of readability, I have provided *selective illustrations* from various translations in support of generalizations that I make. I want my readers to see what I am talking about, but I have made no attempt to be exhaustive. Also, I want my claims to be understood as applying to the Bible translation into English, specifically; I am not qualified to speak to the special issues that arise in translating the Bible into a newly codified language on the mission field.

I have tried to avoid the repetitions that reviewers noticed in my first book (generally not in a critical way). However, I also need to record that a philosophy of translation is a whole system of interlocking components. If one starts with the premise that the actual words of the Bible do not need to be reproduced in translation, a host of additional characteristics follows from that premise. It is not surprising, therefore, that the issue of retaining or departing from the words of the original surfaces in a number of the chapters of this book.

No outcome for my authorial efforts would be more welcome to me than to see many readers reach the position of an e-mailer who wrote the following in response to my first book on Bible translation:

> When I bowed to the pressure of friends to use a dynamic equivalent translation, I felt that my confidence in the scriptures was ripped away. Your book made me think about things I had never thought about before. . . . This may seem like a strange statement, but I feel like someone has literally given my Bible back to me and given me confidence that I can know what the scripture says.

14

# PART ONE

# Overview of Issues

The issues underlying Bible translation have always been momentous, technical, and complex. But until the mid-twentieth century, English Bible translators worked within a consensus regarding the goals and methods of Bible translation. Translators had a clear and relatively simple picture in their minds of what they wanted to achieve. Certainly they did not operate in a context of two rival translation philosophies that prevails today.

Everything changed with the advent of dynamic equivalence as a theory and practice of English Bible translation. Part 1 of this book provides initial clarity to a complex field.

# 1

# Understanding English Bible Translation

THE TRANSLATION SCENE has been in a state of flux for at least a decade. Important developments have occurred since the publication of my first book on English Bible translation, *The Word of God in English*, and this book takes those developments into account.

With a suddenness that remains a mystery, in the middle of the last century principles of translation that had been virtually unchallenged for centuries suddenly became passé for a majority of translators. A new "orthodoxy" swept the field, and much of what I say in this book will be a critique of that philosophy.

With the dawn of the current century, the new "orthodoxy" itself lost its position of unquestioned dominance. To many Bible readers it is no longer self-evident that translators should feel free to give English readers a substitute for the actual words of the original Hebrew and Greek texts. The premise that readers and market research should determine how the biblical text is translated has become highly suspect for many Bible readers. Even readers who continue to prefer dynamic equivalent translations are generally better informed about what kind of Bible they hold in their hands than they were a decade ago.

The translation scene is not only in transition; it is also highly splintered. On one side, dynamic equivalent translations can be plotted on an arc of increasing boldness in departing from what the original biblical text actually says, starting with the NIV and culminating in *The Message*. This family of translations is itself so diverse that it has produced the phenomenon of a destabilized Bible.[1]

On the other end of the continuum, several essentially literal translations have recently appeared and have together diminished the stature that the NIV had enjoyed for three decades. D. A. Carson has correctly identified the rise of linguistic conservatism as one of the new developments of the past quarter century.[2]

### Defining the Terms of the Debate

The best quick introduction to the issues involved in English Bible translation today is a listing of the concepts that underlie translation, accompanied by definitions of the key terms. Virtually all of these terms originated in the last half century, a fact that signals the degree to which English Bible translation entered a new era in the middle of the twentieth century.

- *Receptor language*: the language into which a text written in a foreign language is translated.
- *Donor language*: the original language in which a text is written.
- *Native language*: synonymous with *donor language*—the original language in which a text is written.
- *Dynamic equivalent*: a meaning in the receptor language that is equivalent to (but not identical with) a meaning in a native-language text; for example, the "heart" as the modern way of denoting the essence of a person, especially the emotions, which for the ancients was situated in the kidneys.

- *Dynamic equivalence*: a theory of translation based on the premise that whenever something in the native-language text is foreign or unclear to a contemporary reader, the original text should be translated in terms of a dynamic equivalent.

- *Functional equivalent*: something in the receptor language that differs from what the original text says but that serves the same function in the receptor language; for example, "first fruits" translated as "special offering."

- *Functional equivalence*: a theory of translation that favors replacing a statement in the original text with a functional equivalent whenever the original phraseology or reference is obscure for a modern reader in the receptor language; for example, "holy kiss" translated as "hearty handshake" because the latter is how Christians in Western cultures extend greetings to each other today.

- *Equivalent effect*: translating in such a way as to produce the same effect on readers of the translation as the original text produced on its native-language readers; for example, *The Message* gives the image of "daughters as shapely and bright as fields of wildflowers" as producing the same effect as the original text's image of "daughters like corner pillars cut for the structure of a palace." (Ps. 144:12)

- *Formal equivalence*: a theory of translation that favors reproducing the form or language of the original text, not just its meaning. In its stricter form, this theory of translation espouses reproducing even the syntax and word order of the original; the formula *word for word translation* often implies this stricter definition of the concept.

- *Verbal equivalent*: a word or combination of words in the receptor language that most closely corresponds to a word in the original, native-language text.

- *Essentially literal translation*: a translation that strives to translate the exact words of the original-language text but

19

not in such a rigid way as to violate the normal rules of language and syntax in the receptor language.

- *Linguistic conservatism*: as applied to Bible translation, a general orientation toward language that would seek to *conserve* the actual words of the original text as much as possible; an implied contrast to the "liberalism" of dynamic equivalence, which does not feel bound to reproduce the actual Hebrew and Greek words of the original.

- *Transparent text*: this means two opposite things, and for that very reason the term has become devalued and misleading, even though it continues to be widely used by dynamic equivalent advocates. A text is *transparent to the modern or contemporary reader* when it is immediately understandable in the receptor language; this is the goal of dynamic equivalent translations. A translation is *transparent to the original text* when it reproduces the language, expressions, and customs of the original text; this is the goal of an essentially literal translation.

- *Target audience*: the audience that a translation committee and publisher expect to be the chief market for a translation. Translation committees that consciously bring a target audience into their enterprise make translation decisions based on their desire to appeal to the target audience that they envision.

## What the Terms Tell Us and Don't Tell Us

The definitions in the preceding section of this chapter provide a good introduction to the field of modern translation theory and practice. The terms do a good job of revealing where we currently stand with English Bible translation.

We should note first the dominance of the word *equivalence*. This was a brand-new word on the translation scene when it was introduced in the mid-twentieth century. There was no comparable dominating word for translation before Eugene Nida popularized the new philosophy of translation, but it is pretty clear that the word that translators would have used to describe their practice up to that point was *correspondence.* What translators formerly did was find the *correspondent English words* for the words of the original.

What is significant about the rise of the word *equivalence* as the dominant term? The significance lies in the fact that the word was popularized by Eugene Nida and his followers. While the word *need* not imply license, as used by dynamic equivalent proponents, it *does* imply a loose attitude toward preserving the words of the original text of the Bible. As used by the people who elevated it to the main term in translation theory, translating the Bible into something *equivalent to* the original text stands in implied contrast to translating it into something that *corresponds to* or is *identical with* the words of the original (subject of course to the changes required by translation from one language into another).

We might ask further what the word *dynamic* is doing in the formula. The phrase has become so common that we scarcely note what an odd adjective *dynamic* is in this context. It is mainly an honorific term—dynamic in contrast to the allegedly static or dead products of essentially literal translators. But in this context the word *dynamic* actually means something in addition, namely, a spirit of freedom or exemption from the need to reproduce the actual words of the original in an English translation.

The terms currently in fashion have the pernicious effect of privileging dynamic equivalence over the rival theory of translation. Consider the formula *verbal equivalence.* This would be innocuous and even helpful if it meant "finding the equivalent English word for the word in the original." The problem is that the word *equivalent* has already been co-opted by dynamic equivalent advocates. It carries the connotation of being *a substitute for* rather than *corresponding to* the words of the original biblical text.

We also need to note how inadequate—to the point of being misleading—the terms *dynamic equivalence* and *functional equivalence* are as descriptors of what translations bearing those names actually do with the original text. In fact, only a small

21

amount—almost a statistically insignificant quantity—of what we find in modern dynamic equivalent translations is a matter of finding an equivalent for something in the original. What these translations *mainly* do is beyond that parameter, consisting of such things as changing syntax and word order, adding exegesis and interpretive commentary to the text, simplifying the content of the original text, removing figurative language from sight, producing a colloquial style for the English Bible, and adapting the translation to the expectations of a target audience. None of these activities can be honestly construed as finding an equivalent for difficult words and phrases in the original text of the Bible.

Realistically, the prevailing terminology will not change any time soon. So we need to use the terms in a "state of high alert." Many of the terms are misleading. They also stack the deck in favor of modern translation theories and against traditional understandings of what English Bible translation should be.

# 2

# QUESTIONS AND ANSWERS ABOUT
# ENGLISH BIBLE TRANSLATION

THE ISSUES SURROUNDING English Bible translation are complex. Much of the writing on the subject is so technical that laypeople might well despair of ever understanding the process. In this chapter I will clarify matters by asking and answering a series of questions that frequently surface in regard to English Bible translation. In answering the questions in my own voice, I have pictured myself as responding to questions posed by an interviewer.

1) *Isn't all translation interpretation? If so, aren't essentially literal and dynamic equivalent translations basically the same?*

The favorite motto of dynamic equivalent translators is that "all translation is interpretation." The statement is so misleading that an immediate moratorium should be called on its use.

There is only one sense in which *all* translation is interpretation, and it is not what dynamic equivalent translators usually mean by their cliché. All translation is *lexical or linguistic* interpretation. That is, translators must decide what English word or phrase most closely corresponds to a given word of the original text. I myself do not believe that "interpretation" is the best word by which to name this process, but inasmuch as it requires a "judgment call" on the part of translators, there is something *akin to* interpretation when translators decide whether, for example, the Israelites were led through the wilderness or the desert.

All translation is "interpretation" on the lexical level. But this is the least of what excites dynamic equivalent translators. In fact, they are often impatient with finding the right corresponding word and eager to interpret the meaning of a word or phrase for the allegedly ignorant modern reader.

2) *What do dynamic equivalent translators primarily mean when they speak of all translation being interpretation?*

They primarily mean interpretation of the content of a statement—in other words, exegesis and commentary. For example, *lexical* interpretation of Psalm 23:5b yields the translation "you anoint my head with oil." A typical move by dynamic equivalent translators is to translate that statement as "you welcome me as an honored guest" (GNB). What I have labeled lexical interpretation has actually been bypassed in the second rendition, since the translators who produced it make no claim that the words *honored guest* appear in the original poem. The translators have interpreted the metaphoric meaning of the image of the anointed head. The two types of interpretation that I have noted belong to different realms and cannot accurately be placed on the same continuum.

3) *What's so objectionable about the motto "all translation is interpretation"?*

It is objectionable because its effect is to conceal a basic difference that exists between the rival translation philosophies. The sleight of hand that dynamic equivalent translations hope to perform with their cliché "all translation is interpretation" is to conceal the irreconcilable divergence that exists between retaining the words of the original and substituting an interpretation of meaning in place of those words. The hoped-for effect of the

motto is to imply something like the following: "See—all translation is interpretation, and the liberties that dynamic equivalent
translators take with the original are just part of the normal
work of translation."

Well, those liberties are *not* a necessary part of translation.
Dynamic equivalence introduced a new type of interpretation into
the translation process—a type that essentially literal translators
regard as license. To remove the imagery of the statement "he who
has clean hands and a pure heart" (Ps. 24:4, ESV and others) and
replace it with the statement "those who do right for the right
reasons" (CEV) is to do something with the text that was never
regarded as normal translation practice until the appearance of
dynamic equivalence. All translation is emphatically *not* interpretation as we find it in the second translation quoted above.

**4) Are the labels "dynamic equivalence" and "functional
equivalence" good descriptors?**

No; they are as misleading as the motto "all translation is interpretation." The newer term *functional equivalence* is even more
deceptive than its predecessor, and it is no wonder that enthusiasts
for that approach have latched onto the new label.

Both labels name a process of finding an equivalent in the receptor language for a statement composed in the donor or native
language. Functional equivalence seeks something in the receptor
language that produces the same *effect* (and therefore allegedly
serves the same *function*) as the original statement, no matter how
far removed the new statement might be from the original.

For example, in searching for a metaphor to express how delight-
ful he finds God's law, the poet in Psalm 19:10 landed on "sweeter
also than honey / and drippings from the honeycomb" (most translations). A dynamic equivalent translator asks, now what does someone
in modern Western society find as tasteful as the ancient poet found
honey to be? What in modern experience serves the same *function*
as honey in the category of "something that tastes sweet?" One
translator's answer: "You'll like it better than strawberries in spring,
/ better than red, ripe strawberries" (MESSAGE).

In slight contrast, *dynamic equivalence* widens the scope beyond functional equivalence. Dynamic equivalence is not primarily interested in corresponding *effect*. Instead, dynamic equivalence is interested in finding equivalent *words or expressions* for the original even while departing from the terms used by the biblical author. For example, if the original says "Lord of hosts," dynamic equivalent translators judge that "Lord Almighty" is an adequate lexical equivalent for the original. If the original says "the hearts of the people melted and became as/like water" (all translations that render Joshua 7:5 literally), the other philosophy thinks that a suitable equivalent of the metaphor is "the Israelite army felt discouraged" (CEV) or "the Israelites . . . lost their courage" (NCV) or "their courage melted away" (NLT).

**5) What makes the labels "dynamic equivalence" and "functional equivalence" objectionable?**

Those labels cover only a fraction of what the translators actually do during the process of translation. Correspondingly, the activities that fall into these two categories constitute a relatively small part of what I discuss in this book. Dynamic equivalent translators smuggle in a huge agenda of further activities that have little to do with finding an equivalent for something in the original text. Here is a list of activities that make up the major portion of what dynamic equivalent translators do:

- make the style of the English Bible as contemporary and colloquial (or nearly so) as it is possible to make it;
- change figurative language into direct statement;
- add interpretive commentary in an attempt to make the Bible immediately understandable to a modern reader;
- replace theological vocabulary with everyday vocabulary (true of some but not all dynamic equivalent translations);
- reduce the vocabulary level of the original and of traditional English translations;

- shorten the syntax of the original and/or traditional English translations;
- bring masculine gender references into line with modern feminist preferences.

Very little of the process I have just described involves finding equivalent terminology or "functions" for the original text. My objection to the labels *dynamic equivalence* and *functional equivalence*, therefore, is that they are misleading and deceptive as descriptors of the phenomenon that they are designed to name.

6) *Is the claim true that essentially literal translation is no more than transliteration?*

The claim was made in print by Mark Strauss in a review of my earlier book.[1] (Strauss coauthored a book that makes the opposite claim that all translation—even literal translation—is a form of paraphrase.[2]) A transliteration of Psalm 32:1 reads, "Blessedness of forgiven of transgression, covered of sin." An essentially literal translation is totally different: "Blessed is the one whose transgression is forgiven, whose sin is covered." The charge that essentially literal translators "forget that [the process involves] translation rather than transcription" should be labeled for what it is—frivolous and irresponsible.[3]

7) *Is it true that linguistic theory has made it obsolete to speak of the difference between what the original text "says" and what it "means?"*

No, linguistics has not proven that. The only kernel of truth in the statement is that meaning is ordinarily embodied not in individual words but in more complex word combinations such as phrases, clauses, and sentences. The exception would be in a one-word communication, where the single word embodies the meaning.

The attempt to discredit the distinction between what a passage in the Bible says and what it means is yet another way in which dynamic equivalent translators attempt to phrase the issues

27

in such a way as to make it appear that all translation is really a version of dynamic equivalence. To clarify the matter, we can compare the two columns in Chart 2.1. The left column translates the words of the original into English, while the right substitutes something in place of the words of the original.

**Chart 2:1 What a Text Says vs. What It Means**

| "my joy and crown" (Phil. 4:1) | "how happy you make me, and how proud I am of you" (GNB) |
|---|---|
| "the keepers of the house tremble" (Eccl. 12:3) | "your body will grow feeble" (CEV); or "your limbs will tremble with age" (NLT) |
| "set a guard . . . over my mouth" (Ps. 141:3) | "take control of what I say" (NLT); or "help me control my tongue" (NCV) |

It does not take the proverbial rocket scientist to see that the left column gives us what the original text says: *crown, keepers of the house, guard*. It is equally clear what the original does *not* say: *happy, proud, body, limbs, grow feeble, control, what I say*. Well, then, what do the terms used in the right column represent? They are translators' interpretations of the *meanings* of the words and/or statements in the right column.

The commonsense distinction between what a passage *says* and what it *means* is completely valid, and we should not allow the high-flown technical jargon of linguistics deter us from seeing what is plain to us. The relevance of this to Bible translation is that essentially literal translations give us what the original text *says* (to the extent that translation into English allows), while dynamic equivalent translations regularly remove what the original text says in deference to an interpretation of what it *means*. As biblical scholar Raymond Van Leeuwen states, "It is hard to know what the Bible *means* when we are uncertain about what it *says*."[4]

In making the distinction between what a text says and what it means, I need to guard against leaving the impression that what a text says is not laden with meaning. I am talking about what a translation committee puts before its readers. Essentially literal translators expect readers to determine the meanings that are present in what the original text says. Dynamic equivalent translators sometimes sneer at essentially literal translations as being unconcerned with meaning. The issue rather is that essentially literal translations expect readers to do what the original authors expected them to do—ascertain the meaning from the data that the original text provides.

8) *What is the most commendable thing that can be said about dynamic equivalent translations?*

The most commendable thing is the goal of the translators to render the Bible understandable to modern readers. We need to give credit where credit is due: dynamic equivalent translators want readers to understand the content of the Bible.

9) *Isn't that a sufficient reason to endorse dynamic equivalent translation?*

It is not. The goal of being immediately understandable to a modern reader is inevitably in competition with other goals. Another way of saying this is that dynamic equivalence comes laden with problems that offset the exemplary goal of being easily understandable to a modern reader.

To begin, the readily understandable text is often not even what the Bible says. As the era of dynamic equivalence continues to unfold, the Bible-reading public is farther and farther removed from the biblical text. Many regular Bible readers do not know what the original text of the Bible says because they have used a translation that shields them from encountering what the original text says. They have accepted a substitute. Of course these readers do not know this. They *think* that Luke 1:69 reads, "He has sent us a mighty Savior" (NLT), whereas it actually reads, "He has raised up a horn of salvation for us" (literal translations).

In many quarters, readability has been elevated to an importance that it should never be accorded. What good is readability if the result is not what the biblical writers said?

29

## 10) What is the most objectionable aspect of dynamic equivalence as a method of Bible translation?

There are actually two "strongest" cases against dynamic equivalence. The first is the syndrome of variability among translations and the destabilized text that results. When a dynamic equivalent translator shows us just his or her preferred translation, the case is so plausible that it seems perverse to object to it. But problems set in when we start comparing that preferred translation to other things.

The first of these things is what the original text of the Bible actually says. If a dynamic equivalent translation differs from the original text (as it often does), we have a problem with accuracy. The second broader context that is often damning for dynamic equivalence is the variation that exists within the dynamic equivalent family of translations.

Psalm 78:33 can serve as an illustration. Suppose we read the first line of that verse in the NLT: "So he ended their lives in failure." That would seem to be innocuous. But suppose we want to make sure that this is what the original text says. If we consult English Bibles that give us that, we have every reason to be worried. What the poet said was that God ended the days of the wicked "like a breath [or vapor]" (ESV, AMP). Well, which is it—"in failure" or "like a breath"? In a situation like this, a reader *ought* to be able to trust a translation to give us an English version of what the original author wrote.

If, in turn, we consult other translations, we find our problem multiplied: "cut their lives short" (CEV); "in futility" (NIV, NASB, NKJV); "come to nothing" (NLV); "in calamity" (NEB); "in emptiness" (REB). *Failure, futility, emptiness, calamity, cut short*—I myself cannot conceive of how someone can look at such variability and conclude that it is an acceptable state of affairs for Bible translation. There are two problems here: (1) most of the translations do not give us the original author's image of breath or vapor, and (2) what they substitute in place of it is contradictory to other translations, not all of which can be accurate.

The variability that I have noted gives the lie to a dynamic equivalent argument that seems plausible until we look at it more closely. Dynamic equivalent translators feel entitled to change what the biblical authors wrote because they know more than most Bible readers know. As Eugene Nida put it, "The average reader is usually much less capable of making correct judgments . . . than is the translator, who can make use of the best scholarly judgments."[5] But the experts' superior scholarship does us absolutely no good when it comes to producing a reliable translation if the experts cannot agree among themselves as to what the original text means!

**11)** *What is the other major case against dynamic equivalence?*

It is that in the overwhelming number of cases where dynamic equivalent translators change what the biblical authors wrote, *the authors of the Bible could have phrased it that way* but did not. The writer of Ecclesiastes had the resources to say "your teeth will decay" (Eccl. 12:3, CEV), but instead he wrote, "The grinders cease because they are few." Amos could have said, "I gave you empty stomachs in every city" (Amos 4:6, NIV) or "hunger" (NLT), but instead he said "cleanness of teeth" (literal translation).

Dynamic equivalent translators do not set out to be arrogant vis-à-vis the authors of the Bible, but we need to be forthright. In their actual practices, dynamic equivalent translators show that they think they can do a better job of communicating God's message than the original authors did. When translators remove a biblical author's metaphor, in that very act they show that they believe the biblical author did not "get it right": the author used a metaphor and should not have. When translators add interpretive commentary to what the original text says, they show that they believe the biblical author should have done more than he did. Whatever we might call this, it is not humility before the biblical authors and text.

Neither do dynamic equivalent translators show humility toward their readers. I am offended anew every time I read the statement in the preface to the NIV that "for most readers today" the

31

phrases *the Lord of hosts* and *God of hosts* "have little meaning." I find those two epithets for God hugely evocative. But even if I did not, it is presumptuous for a translation committee to decide whether something in the Bible is meaningful for a reader.

**12)** *Does any usefulness remain for dynamic equivalent translations?*

Yes. I use them as commentaries instead of translations. When I explicate a text, I first consult the ESV, then the NASB, then the NKJV. Those translations give me confidence that I know what the original says. If I find a given statement difficult to understand, I have a look at dynamic equivalent translations to get a feel for what the text might mean. Sometimes the dynamic equivalent translations are in general agreement, and sometimes they differ widely. But this degree of variance is what I am likely to find among commentators, too, so I do not find the variance unsettling if I put the translations into the category of commentaries, whereas that same range is very unsettling to me if I am looking for a *translation* that is supposed to inform me of what the original actually says.

I sometimes encounter the viewpoint that when a dynamic equivalent translation offers a good interpretation of a biblical passage, it has been "a good translation" in that particular instance. This is an incorrect verdict; it has been a good *commentary* in that instance. To the extent that the translation has prevented a reader from seeing what the biblical author actually wrote, it has been a bad *translation*.

**13)** *Is it possible to highlight the differences between the rival translation philosophies at a glance?*

Chart 2.2 names the points on which the two kinds of translation differ and then gives an illustration of the difference. The left column gives essentially literal renditions, while the right column illustrates dynamic equivalence. Since I want the emphasis to fall on the *type* of translation, I have not given the specific translations from which my examples come.

**Chart 2.2 How the Rival Translation Philosophies Differ**

| | |
|---|---|
| 1) Fidelity to the words of the original vs. feeling free to substitute something in place of those words (Ps. 90:17): | |
| "Establish the work of our hands upon us." (What the verse actually says.) | "Give us success in what we do"; or "Let all go well for us." |
| 2) Limiting the process of translation to translating the words of the original vs. adding explanatory commentary beyond what the original authors wrote (Ps. 23:5): | |
| "You anoint my head with oil, my cup overflows." | "*You honor me* by anointing my head with oil. My cup overflows *with blessings.*" (Italics show what the translators have added to the biblical text.) |
| 3) Retaining the concrete vocabulary of the original vs. replacing the concretion with an abstraction (Luke 22:42): | |
| "Father, if you are willing, remove this cup from me." | "Father, if it can be done, take away what must happen to Me." |
| 4) Retaining a figure of speech in the original vs. removing a figure of speech (Col. 3:9): | |
| "Seeing you have put off the old self . . . and put on the new self." (Garment metaphor retained.) | "You have left your old sinful life . . . and begun to live the new life." (Garment metaphor removed.) |
| 5) Passing on to the reader the ambiguity/multiple meanings of the original vs. resolving the ambiguity/multiplicity in a single direction (2 Thess. 3:5): | |
| "The love of God . . ." (Can be both the believer's love for God and God's love for the believer.) | "God's love . . ." (The double meanings reduced to one.) |
| 6) Producing a relatively high level of vocabulary and syntax vs. producing a simplified level of vocabulary and syntax (Eccl. 3:11–12): | |
| "He has made everything beautiful in its time. Also, he has put eternity into man's heart, yet so that he cannot find out what God has done from the beginning to the end." | "God makes everything happen at the right time. Yet none of us can ever fully understand all he has done, and he puts questions in our minds about the past and the future." |
| 7) Producing an English Bible that possesses a dignified and relatively formal style vs. producing a colloquial Bible (Eccl. 11:9): | |
| "Rejoice, O young man, in your youth, and let your heart cheer you in the days of your youth. Walk in the ways of your heart and the sight of your eyes." | "Young people, it's wonderful to be young! Enjoy every minute of it. Do everything you want to do; take it all in." |
| 8) Retaining traditional theological vocabulary vs. avoiding traditional theological vocabulary (1 Tim. 2:6): | |
| "Who gave himself as a ransom for all." | "He gave his life to set all men free." |

# PART TWO

# The Story of English Bible Translation

There are several reasons why it is important to be familiar with the history of English Bible translation. The first is that this story is one of the most exciting adventure stories in English Christendom. The second is that it is salutary to know at what price—even the price of martyrdom—the English Bible was originally produced.

Additionally, the history of English Bible translation provides a context for understanding English Bible translation in our own time. It tells us how we arrived where we find ourselves today.

The purpose of Part 2 of this book is not only informational. It is designed to delineate the main tradition of English Bible translation and to show that the dominance of dynamic equivalent translations is a recent phenomenon and a deviation from what prevailed for four centuries.

# 3

# LAYING THE FOUNDATION

THERE HAVE BEEN two major eras of English Bible translation. The first is the sixteenth century. The forerunner of this tradition was the Wycliffe Bible (1380), produced by followers of John Wycliffe. It was written in Middle English and was based on the Latin Vulgate (not the original Hebrew and Greek). Produced before the invention of the printing press, it circulated in handwritten manuscript form only. It was so prized that merely using a copy for one day cost the price of a load of hay, while purchasing a copy would take four times the average annual salary of a country parson.[1]

## William Tyndale: Founder of English Bible Translation

The archaic language of sixteenth-century translations leads many people to call it "old English," but that is a misnomer. Sixteenth-century English was modern English, as distinct from its predecessors Old English and Middle English. The tradition of translating the Bible into modern English begins with William Tyndale.

### Tyndale's Life as a Translator

Tyndale (1494–1536) was a linguistic genius whose expertise in seven languages dazzled the scholarly world of his day. Educated at Oxford University and eventually ordained as a priest, he rather quickly came to see translating the Bible into English as his vocation in life.

Because the vernacular Bible was condemned by the Roman Catholic Church, Tyndale did his work of translation while living on the Continent. He finished his translation of the New Testament in 1525, and copies reached England the following year, smuggled in bales of cloth and sacks of flour. Catholic bishops conducted public burnings of the books. Tyndale began work on the Old Testament but was lured out of hiding by a Catholic sympathizer. He was declared a heretic and met his end near Brussels by strangling and burning at the stake in 1535.

For people who have multiple English Bibles on their shelves, it is important to be reminded that the vernacular Bible was begotten in blood. What we take for granted originally seemed impossible.

### What Kind of Translation?

All translation is undergirded by a philosophy of translation. Tyndale did not write a treatise on Bible translation, so we are left to infer what his theory was. There can be no doubt that Tyndale knew that he was doing a pioneering work and that the foundational principles on which he based his translation would be influential to posterity.

Tyndale's first principle was that any translation needs to be a translation of the words of the original Hebrew and Greek of the Old and New Testaments, respectively. This may seem obvious, but it was not obvious before Tyndale's time. The Latin Vulgate had been the assumed starting point for serious Bible study and translation for centuries. We should credit the Catholic Erasmus for his landmark publication of an improved Greek New Testament in 1516. Tyndale's commitment to give the English equivalent of the actual words of the original biblical text also stands as an implied contrast to modern translations that minimize the importance of preserving the words of the original.

A second principle that we can see in Tyndale's translation is devotion to clarity as a leading goal of translation. Scholar David Daniell credits Tyndale with establishing an English "plain style."[2] We need to tread cautiously here. The adjective *plain* can be "clear," or it can mean "common; colloquial." It is true that Tyndale's translation includes a few famous colloquialisms, as when the serpent says to Eve, "Tush, ye shall not die," or when Joseph is called "a luckie felowe."

But the English of Tyndale's New Testament is predominantly a dignified plain style. It is as informal or formal as the original requires. Tyndale's rendition of the famous Beatitudes of Jesus shows this:

> Blessed are the poor in spirit: for theirs is the kingdom of heaven. Blessed are they that mourn: for they shall be comforted. Blessed are the meek: for they shall inherit the earth Blessed are they which hunger and thirst for righteousness: for they shall be filled.[3]

The language in such a passage is simple, but the style is poetic, and the rhetoric is a masterpiece of balance and parallelism. It is not the idiom of the dormitory or the grocery store.

Similarly, the syntax of the following excerpt from the parable of the rich man and Lazarus is complex rather than simple: "And being in hell in torments, he lifted up his eyes and saw Abraham afar off, and Lazarus in his bosom, and he cried and said: father Abraham, have mercy on me, and send Lazarus that he may dip the tip of his finger in water, and cool my tongue: for I am tormented in this flame" (Luke 16:23–24). The language structures here are complex and sophisticated.

From the beginning, Tyndale apparently sensed that the Bible is a special book filled with qualities that set it off from everyday conversation. One of its qualities is an aphoristic beauty that makes it stick in the memory if it is translated in keeping with the contours of the original text. Tyndale successfully combined clarity with an aphoristic flair that raises his translation higher than the language of the street. Eighty percent of Tyndale's translation found its way into the King James Version of the parts of the Bible that Tyndale had translated, and surely no one would claim that the King James Bible sounds like everyday conversation.

---

William Tyndale influenced not only the subsequent history of Bible translation but also the English language itself. Many of the most famous aphorisms in our language originally appeared in Tyndale's English translation of the Bible. Here is a short list:

- Be not weary in well doing.
- Am I my brother's keeper?
- The salt of the earth.
- The signs of the times.
- A law unto themselves.
- The spirit is willing, but the flesh is weak.
- Fight the good fight.
- With God all things are possible.
- The patience of Job.

---

Not only did Tyndale refuse to conform his translation *stylistically* to the language of the workplace; he also refused to accept the limitations of *vocabulary* that he found. He thus coined English words when he found it necessary to do so. Of special importance in this regard are the words that Tyndale introduced into the English language in order to do justice to the theological content of the Bible. Examples include *passover, intercession, scapegoat,* and *atonement.* These are doubtless "big words," new to Tyndale's original readers, but Tyndale insisted on them because the theological complexity of the Bible required them.

### Tyndale's Legacy

William Tyndale is the fountainhead of English Bible translation. The patterns that he laid down remained the norm for five centuries and are still the model for many modern translations. One scholar concludes that the translation of Tyndale "imposed itself on all later versions, down to the present day."[4] We can attribute three specific things to Tyndale's work as a translator.

One is an acknowledgment of the centrality of the vernacular Bible to the health of the Christian church. The original Protestant movement could not have existed without the vernacular Bible. Tyndale famously replied to a Catholic sympathizer that "if God spare my life, ere many years I will cause a boy that driveth the plough shall know more of the Scripture than thou dost." This has been incorrectly interpreted as a comment on Tyndale's English style; it is instead a comment on Tyndale's desire to see the English Bible permeate all of English society.

Tyndale's dream was realized: England became a biblical culture within a few decades of Tyndale's death.[5] Someone who lived through the movement gave this contemporary account:

> It was wonderful to see with what joy the book of God was received, not only among the learneder sort and those that were noted for lovers of the reformation, but generally all England over among all the vulgar and common people; with what greediness God's word was read, and what resort to places where the reading of it was. Everybody that could bought the book and busily read it; or got others to read it to them, if they could not themselves; and diverse among the elderly learned to read on purpose. And even little boys flocked among the rest to hear portions of the Holy Scriptures read.[6]

---

"Tyndale was in the vanguard of the popular English Reformation. . . . The great change that came over England from 1526, the ability of every ordinary man, woman and child to read and hear the whole New Testament in English, accurately rendered, was Tyndale's work. . . . He gave the Bible-reading nation an English plain style. . . . There is truth in the remark 'without Tyndale, no Shakespeare.'" —David Daniell

---

In addition to Tyndale's awareness of the importance of having the Bible accessible to all people in their own language, we can credit him with establishing certain principles of translation. One is a commitment to translate what the original Hebrew and Greek texts say. Another is adherence to the twin virtues of accuracy and clarity. A third is the acceptance of the principle of dignity of expression that raised the biblical style above that of everyday discourse wherever the original required it.[7]

An additional principle is Tyndale's refusal to capitulate to the linguistic and theological abilities of the least educated segments of his society. It is obvious from his translation practices that Tyndale expected the plowboy to rise above the language that he used when talking with his fellow worker or the neighbor across the fence. Tyndale did not conduct market research and then slant his translation to its results. He translated as his considerable scholarly and linguistic abilities told him he needed to, and he then expected his readers to rise to the level required.

## The Triumph of the English Bible

Tyndale was a pioneer working in a virtual vacuum. The English language that he inherited was impoverished, and there was no model for translating the Bible into modern English. Furthermore, he had translated a relatively small portion of the Old Testament when he was martyred. It is no discredit to Tyndale, therefore, to call the ensuing succession of English translations a process of refining what Tyndale had started.

### Between Tyndale and the King James Version

It is not relevant to our purpose here to tell the entire story of English Bible translation during the sixteenth century. The brief history that follows is designed to show three things: (1) the way in which an entire century devoted its energies to translating and reading the English Bible; (2) the way in which successive translations helped to refine and improve the English Bible; (3) the way in which the English Bible transformed the English church and society.

In order to see these things, we need to have the facts before us. Here in brief is the lineage of sixteenth-century translations and their distinctive contributions to the ongoing process of moving toward a definitive English translation:

*Coverdale's Bible* (1535). Miles Coverdale, who had worked as an assistant to Tyndale, produced the first complete Bible in English. It was the first English translation to be approved (though not officially authorized) by the king, Henry VIII, and copies were accordingly chained to desks in cathedrals and churches, where people could read them. Coverdale's Bible was the first to include chapter summaries and marginal notes.

*Matthew's Bible* (1537). "Thomas Matthew" was a pen name for John Rogers, who was a friend of Tyndale and later martyred under the Catholic Queen Mary. His translation was an edited version of the translations of Tyndale and Coverdale. Events had changed so much in just a few years that King Henry VIII, who had earlier approved of the burning of Protestant translations, now officially authorized the new version of the Bible. Matthew's Bible divided the material into chapters and paragraphs (but not verses) and included copious notes and cross-references. The first English concordance was based on this Bible.

*The Great Bible* (1539). We should pause to note that the ferment of translation activity was so great that for a brief span *every two years* saw the appearance of a new translation of the Bible. The Great Bible received its name from its huge size. The title page of the 1540 edition said that "this is the Byble appoynted to the use of the churches," meaning that it was the official Bible for use in the English church. It was chained to "some convenient place" within the churches throughout England. This made such a hit that the king needed to make a proclamation in the very year of the appearance of the Great Bible forbidding its being read aloud during church services.

*The Geneva Bible* (1560). In terms of circulation and influence, this was the major Bible for nearly a century after its appearance. This was partly because of its superiority, and partly because it was the Bible of the English Puritans. As its title implies, the Geneva Bible was produced in Switzerland by Puritan refugees who had fled the persecution of the Catholic Queen Mary. It quickly became the household Bible of English-speaking

Protestants, and it was the Bible most used by Shakespeare and carried to America on the *Mayflower*.

The things that the Geneva Bible introduced into the English Bible tradition included the following: (1) the presence of marginal notes that provided commentary on the biblical text; (2) a smaller size, making it more affordable than its predecessors and giving it a mass appeal as opposed merely to official church sanction; (3) printing in easier-to-read roman typeface rather than black gothic lettering; (4) italicizing of words not in the original text but needed to make sense in English; (5) dividing the text into verses as well as chapters.

*The Bishops' Bible* (1568). The Geneva Bible, being Puritan and radically Protestant in its translation preferences and marginal notes, was distrusted by high church Anglicans and the ruling monarch (Queen Elizabeth). The Bishops' Bible received its title from the fact that it was produced by Anglican clergymen (chiefly bishops). It changed its predecessor the Great Bible only where the latter was linguistically faulty. Although it became the official Anglican Bible, Queen Elizabeth never actually authorized it, and it never successfully rivaled the Geneva Bible.

### Lessons to Be Learned

The triumph of the vernacular Bible in the sixteenth century was not the achievement of an individual but of a whole culture and society. More specifically, it was a triumph of Protestantism. Translating the Bible into English and disseminating it to everyone who wished to read it was the Protestant counterpart of the way in which the building of cathedrals seized the Catholic imagination in the Middle Ages and engaged an entire society.

Not only was the Bible translation movement of the sixteenth century a communal effort in the sense that it activated the energies of a whole nation; it was also a communal triumph in the sense that successive translators consciously built upon and improved their predecessors. A whole process of refinement was going on, and although translators could not have known what was to follow, there was an inner momentum toward the final climax of the King James Version, as we will see in the next chapter. The felicities of phrasing that various translations added to the tradition are as exciting as an adventure story (see boxed item on this subject).

---

The successive translations of the sixteenth century all contributed triumphs of phrasing to the edifice that was under construction. Here are some samples:

- Tyndale: *an eye for an eye; O ye of little faith; there were in the same region shepherds abiding in the field and watching their flock by night; he went out . . . and wept bitterly; give us this day our daily bread; in him we live and move and have our being*
- Coverdale: *the valley of the shadow of death; thou anointest my head with oil; baptized into his death; tender mercies; lovingkindness; respect of persons.*
- Geneva: *smite them hip and thigh; vanity of vanities; my cup runneth over; except a man be born again; comfort ye my people.*

---

Third, the progress of English Bible translation in the sixteenth century shows a close connection between evangelical Protestantism and accessibility to the Bible. It was the presence of the vernacular Bible that made the Protestant Reformation (including its English branch) possible. As Catholic Church officials clearly saw, once people had access to the Bible, Catholicism's control of Christendom would vanish. It did.

The relatively uneducated Protestant martyrs who died under the Catholic Queen Mary were noteworthy for their knowledge of the Bible; as Christopher Hill expresses it, "They took on bishops and scholars, out-argued and out-texted them."[8] Two of the dominant themes of J. W. Martin's book *Religious Radicals in Tudor England* are the close correspondence between radical Protestantism and Bible reading on the one hand and Catholic hostility to Bible reading on the other.[9]

Finally, the widespread dissemination of the English Bible revolutionized not only the church but also English society. The existence of a vernacular Bible was a great spur to literacy, and many children learned to read via the Bible.[10] When Tyndale did his work of translation, the important language of educated people in Europe was Latin, and the English language was in a paltry state. Tyndale gave England the language we know today, and it was hunger for the vernacular Bible that made the English plain style widely known. The very printing of books exploded in the wake of English Bible translation.[11] Scholars correctly speak of how the English Bible produced "a cultural revolution of unprecedented proportions" and "a large national shift."[12]

# 4

# Building on the Foundation

THE PREFACE TO THE Revised Standard Version (1952) claims that the translators aimed to "stay as close to the Tyndale–King James tradition as" they could. The preface to the English Standard Version (2001) similarly claims allegiance to "the Tyndale–King James Legacy." And the preface to the New King James Version (1983) signals its allegiance to "the legacy of the 1611 translators" of the King James Version.

What *is* "the King James tradition?" This chapter aims to answer that question by first exploring the nature of the King James Version of the English Bible and then tracing its influence on a certain family of translations to the present day.

## The King James Version (1611)

Despite all contemporary attempts to debunk the King James Version, it is the supreme English translation of the Bible. This eminence encompasses both its superior qualities as an English Bible and its unparalleled influence on the English-speaking world.

### Producing the King James Version

The King James translation takes its name from the ruling monarch who had just taken the throne in England in 1603, having reigned in Scotland since 1567. The Puritans had high hopes for a sympathetic hearing from the new king, but their hopes were uniformly dashed by King James at the famous Hampton Court Conference of 1604. At the end of the conference, the king pretended to give the Puritans a concession by proposing a new translation of the Bible. It was a move actually fuelled by his dislike of the Puritan Geneva Bible, which he disdainfully put down with the comment at the conference that he had never yet seen "a Bible well translated in English," but "the worst of all" was the Geneva Bible.

The story of the translation process has been told many times and is beyond the scope of this chapter.[1] The concern here is the nature of the translation that resulted from the process. The first thing to note is that the King James Version represented the culmination of nearly a century of profuse Bible translation activity in England. As noted in the preceding chapter, successive sixteenth-century translations kept refining what Tyndale had started. The King James translators reaped the benefits of this refining process. "In a cumulative way," writes Benson Bobrick, "all the virtues of the various translations which preceded it were gathered up."[2]

The translators said as much in the preface to their translation. In it they stated, "Truly (good Christian Reader) we never thought from the beginning, that we should need to make a new translation, nor yet to make of a bad one a good one . . . ; but to make a good one better, or out of many good ones, one principal good one." *One principal good one*—that is what the King James Version was, and the English-speaking world eventually ensured it by the preeminence that it gave to the KJV for three centuries.

Some modern scholars and translators make snide remarks about new translations that are revisions rather than brand new translations, but the KJV stands as a rebuttal to this viewpoint by being a revision rather than a new translation. The KJV was a revision of the Bishops' Bible. Additionally, the translators had a mandate to consult other sixteenth-century translations "when they agree better with the [original] text than the Bishops' Bible."[3] Alister McGrath praises this process as "an outstanding example and embodiment" of the spirit of the Renaissance, whose approach to wisdom was one "in which one generation is nourished and sustained by the intellectual achievements of its predecessors"—a "corporate approach to cultural advance and the enterprise of gaining wisdom."[4]

> "The 'Authorized Version' represents a slow, almost impersonal evolution. For it is, in reality, itself a revision, resting upon earlier versions, and these, in turn, depend in varying degrees upon each other, so that through the gradual exercise of something which approaches natural selection, there has come about, in both diction and phraseology, a true survival of the fittest. . . . The long process of version upon version served (to use Dante's phrase) as 'a sieve for noble words.'" —John Livingston Lowes

One of the primary translation principles that we can infer from the actual translation is the principle that in our own day has become known as verbal equivalence (also known as formal equivalence). This means that the translators strove to find an English equivalent for the actual words of the original Hebrew and Greek texts. In his book-length study on the King James Bible and its tradition, Alister McGrath writes as follows:

A careful study of the way in which the King James Bible translates the Greek and Hebrew originals suggests that the translators felt obliged to:

1) Ensure that every word in the original was rendered by an English equivalent;
2) Make it clear when they added any words to make the sense clearer, or to lead to better English syntax. . . .
3) Follow the basic word order of the original wherever possible.[5]

McGrath adds that "this general approach to translation can be shown to have been widespread in the late Middle Ages," beginning with the Wycliffite translations.

A second principle that guided the translators was dignity and even eloquence of language and phraseology. The KJV appeared at the height of the era when the English language was in its greatest flowering. The three teams of translators who produced the translation represented the best Hebrew and Greek scholarship of their day, but they also absorbed a love of the English language from the culture in which they had grown up.

The key concept here is that the translators were *naturally* rather than self-consciously literary in what they produced. As McGrath observes, "The king's translators achieved literary distinction precisely because they were not deliberately pursuing it. Aiming at truth, they achieved what later generations recognized as beauty and elegance. . . . Paradoxically, elegance was achieved by accident."[6] This should not obscure, however, that the translators consciously adopted a prevailingly formal rather than colloquial style.

The KJV was first published in 1611. Debunkers have made far too much of the fact that it was not an immediate sensation. It *was* a success, and within a few decades it supplanted the Geneva Bible as the dominant English version. Although the KJV eventually came to be known as the Authorized Version—the AV—it did not in fact receive the advantage of being officially sanctioned by either the king or the clerical hierarchy (even though the title page claimed that it was "appointed to be read in Churches").

### Qualities of the King James Bible

The traits that resulted from the process described above are universally acknowledged. One is beauty of language. As David Daniell summarizes the matter, "The language of KJV is beautiful. Right through the sixty-six books of the Bible, . . . phrases of lapidary beauty have been deeply admired."[7] That many of these phrases were inherited from earlier translations is irrelevant; the point is that it was the KJV that codified these triumphs of phraseology. In the words of one scholar, the King James Bible represents "the harvesting or refining of the previous century's experiences in translating the Bible into English."[8]

A second feature of the KJV is variety of style. The linguistic dignity and beauty already noted are often allowed to obscure the actual range of styles present in the KJV. The fact that the KJV language became so familiar has incorrectly created the impression that it is uniformly eloquent or grand. On the contrary, scholars regularly claim that 90 percent of the words in the KJV are of native Anglo-Saxon origin.[9] The King James vocabulary of six to eight thousand words is modest when compared to Milton's thirteen thousand and Shakespeare's twenty thousand or more.

The King James style is so flexible that it can give us homespun simplicity and realism in its narrative sections: "Then Jacob gave Esau bread and pottage of lentiles; and he did eat and drink, and rose up, and went his way: thus Esau despised his birthright" (Gen. 25:34). It can also give us the very touchstone of poetry: "He maketh me to lie down in green pastures: he leadeth me beside the still waters" (Ps 23:2). It can be eloquent where the original is eloquent: "But will God indeed dwell on the earth? behold, the heaven and heaven of heavens cannot contain thee; how much less this that I have builded?" (1 Kings 8:27).

---

The stream of commendatory descriptions of the King James Version is virtually without end. Here is a sampling:

- "A polished collation, a refinement of a century's translating, a book . . . both clear and rich."—Adam Nicolson
- "Compared with its predecessors, the King James version shows a superb faculty of selection and combination, a sure instinct for betterment." —Charles Butterworth
- "Stylistically superior to all other versions."—John Ciardi
- "The noblest monument of English prose."—John Livingston Lowes
- "Unquestionably the most beautiful book in the world."—H. L. Mencken
- "If everything else in our language should perish it would alone suffice to show the whole extent of its beauty and power."—Thomas Macaulay

---

The King James translators were also masters of rhythm. This, too, they inherited from their culture, which was still an oral

51

culture in which the spoken word counted for a lot. In addition, the fact that English was still an inflected language meant that unaccented suffixes like *eth* ("prayeth") and *est* ("givest") were available to help keep the meter flowing in regular meter. The result is a smooth and mellifluous flow of words and phrases, in contrast to the staccato effect of some modern translations: "Beareth all things, believeth all things, hopeth all things, endureth all things" (1 Cor. 13:7).

The literary qualities noted above are most readily attested by the memorability of the King James Version. A list of common sayings or proverbs in the English language is largely from the King James Bible: "fire and brimstone" (Ps. 11:6); "the root of the matter" (Job 19:28); "pride goeth before . . . a fall" (Prov. 16:18); "a thorn in the flesh" (2 Cor. 12:7); "gave up the ghost" (Mark 15:37); "at their wit's end" (Ps. 107:27); "labour of love" (1 Thess. 1:3); "clear as crystal" (Rev. 22:1); "house divided against itself" (Matt. 12:25); "see eye to eye" (Isa. 52:8). Not least of the influences of the KJV was the way in which it helped to shape the English language.

It is no accident that the KJV "held undisputed sway in the English-speaking world for more than two centuries."[10] It possesses the qualities of excellence that enabled it to rise to the top and maintain people's loyalty once it had achieved its position of dominance.

### Summary: The King James Version

The foregoing account of the King James Version is not merely of historical interest. The KJV bequeathed a legacy of enduring traits that make it a standard of excellence in every age of English Bible translation. Even though its language is archaic for a modern reader, and even though scholarship has generated resources undreamed of by the KJV translators, the underlying principles of the translation remain valid. They include the following:

- a conviction that "an accurate translation is, by and large, a literal and formal translation" of the original text;[11]
- combined simplicity and majesty of language, with the proportions of each determined by the original text;
- appropriation of the contributions of preceding English Bible translations instead of striving for innovation;
- acknowledgment of the importance of smooth rhythm and meter in both poetry and prose.

## The King James Tradition

It is untrue that the outmoded language of the KJV, along with its deficient scholarly underpinnings, means that it should be relegated to the museum of dead books. As just noted, the King James Bible encompassed certain principles that can serve as both a model and an inspiration for translators in any era. A succession of translations in the KJV lineage proves that this is true. The chief landmarks in this tradition are the following.

*Revised Standard Version* (1946 [NT], 1952 [OT], 1957 [complete], 1971 [revised NT]). The name refers to the fact that this was a revision of the ill-conceived, overly literal and archaic *American Standard Version* of 1901; but the RSV can more accurately be considered to be a revision of the King James Bible. One historian of English Bible translation correctly calls the RSV "the modern American successor" to the KJV—"a thoroughgoing revision of the King James Bible in terms of modern scholarship" that retained "the traditional dignity" of the KJV.[12] The preface to the RSV confirms this, claiming that the translators strove to stand "in the great Tyndale–King James tradition."[13] Next to the KJV, the RSV is the most literary English translation (though some of the literary excellence is based on a tendency toward emendation no longer favored by translators).

*New American Standard Bible* (1971). This translation belongs to the King James tradition, not in its style, which lacks the literary polish of such translations as the RSV and ESV, but by virtue of its devotion to translating the very words of the original.

Although I have placed the NASB in the King James tradition, I note that its preface makes no such connection.

> "There is no doubt that the King James Bible is a model English text. . . . Yet translations eventually require revision, not necessarily because they are defective, but because the language into which they [were] translated itself changes over time. . . . King James's translators honored and made use of the English translations that already lay to hand. . . . The true heirs of the King James translators are those who continue their task today."
> —Alister McGrath

*New King James Version* (1982–1983). The very name of this translation signals its allegiance to the original King James Bible of 1611. According to its preface, the goal of the translators was conceived as "unlocking for today's readers the spiritual treasures found especially in the Authorized Version of the Holy Scriptures." This desire to preserve what was excellent in the KJV extends to both its "majestic and reverent style" and its acceptance of the translation philosophy of "complete equivalence," by which the translators mean faithfulness to the actual words of the original.

*English Standard Version* (2001). The impetus for this translation places it squarely in the King James tradition. That impetus was threefold: (1) a strongly felt need for a more literal translation than the dynamic equivalent movement provides; (2) a desire for a translation possessing more literary flair than the literal but inartistic NASB; (3) a belief that a worthy successor to the KJV needs to be based on more accurate original manuscripts than the New King James Version adopted. The starting point for the translation was the 1971 RSV. The preface to the ESV translation, like others noted above, self-consciously claims "the Tyndale–King James legacy" (also called "the classic mainstream of English Bible translations") as its guiding light.

### Summary: The King James Tradition

Sixteenth-century translations of the Bible laid the foundation for all subsequent English Bible translations. All of these translations led up to the monumental King James Version, whose preface clearly states that the translators built upon the foundation that had been laid. The selective history of translations provided in this chapter shows that further building on the foundation has continued right to the present day.

# 5

# Building on Another
# Foundation

PARADIGM SHIFTS are a predictable feature of the human scene, and often it is not fully evident why a given shift occurs. For a new paradigm to gain acceptance, there needs to be a widespread agreement that the existing paradigm is simply wrong. Once the pendulum begins to swing, no convincing reasons need to be offered for concluding that the old paradigm was untenable. People simply agree with each other that what a previous generation accepted as truth is now deficient.

The mid-twentieth century saw a paradigm shift in the theory and practice of English Bible translation. The preceding two chapters described the foundation of English Bible translation that was laid in the sixteenth century and the tradition that was built on that foundation from the King James Bible of 1611 right to the present moment. In this chapter I will look at the triumph of dynamic equivalence under the format "building on another foundation."

## A Seismic Shift in Bible Translation

As a quick entry into the field, I will simply contrast parallel passages from the first avowed dynamic equivalent translation—the

57

Good News Bible (also published under the title Today's English Version)—with the most recent traditional translation that had appeared at that time—the Revised Standard Version.

### Biblical Narrative in Contrasting Styles

Here is an excerpt from the story of the exchanged birthright between Jacob and Esau as it appears in the RSV (Gen. 25:27–30):

> When the boys grew up, Esau was a skilful hunter, a man of the field, while Jacob was a quiet man, dwelling in tents. Isaac loved Esau, because he ate of his game; but Rebekah loved Jacob. Once when Jacob was boiling pottage, Esau came in from the field, and he was famished. And Esau said to Jacob, "Let me eat some of that red pottage, for I am famished!"

That would have sounded thoroughly familiar to a Bible reader in the middle of the twentieth century. But if the same reader had picked up a copy of the new Good News Bible at the local Christian bookstore, he or she would have sensed something very different about the new translation:

> The boys grew up, and Esau became a skilled hunter, a man who loved the outdoors, but Jacob was a quiet man who stayed at home. . . . One day while Jacob was cooking some bean soup, Esau came in from hunting. He was hungry and said to Jacob, "I'm starving; give me some of that red stuff."

The most obviously new trait is that this is a colloquial translation. The slightly formal expression of the RSV is here rendered as close to modern informal conversation as possible. "I am famished" has become "I'm starving." "Let me eat" has become a curt "give me." "Red pottage" has become "red stuff."

Part of the modernizing consists of giving a reader the modern equivalent of details in the ancient world in which Jacob and Esau actually lived. In the RSV, Jacob is said to dwell in tents; in the GNB, he "stayed at home." In the former case,

58

readers are transported in imagination to the nomadic world of the ancient Near East; in the latter, they remain right in modern suburbia.

Finally, there is just a hint of something that would become more and more pronounced as the dynamic equivalent movement evolved, namely, the impulse to add explanatory material right in the translation. To speak of Esau as "a man of the field" gives modern readers pause; they need to figure out from the context or become educated in the world of Genesis in order to realize that this means that Esau spent a lot of time hunting game in the open countryside. We do not need to figure that out from the GNB's rendition "a man who loved the outdoors." But of course the latter introduces totally misleading and irrelevant data into the picture: there are many ways to love the outdoors having nothing to do with the story of Esau, and to render it as the GNB does misses the link between hunting and the "field" where animals could be hunted. In our culture, a person who loves the outdoors is likely to be a hiker or gardener.

### Biblical Poetry in Contrasting Styles

A comparison of how the two translations render the first verse of Psalm 1 reinforces what we have seen in the passage of prose narrative. The RSV stays very close to its KJV model:

> Blessed is the man
> who walks not in the counsel of the wicked,
> nor stands in the way of sinners,
> nor sits in the seat of scoffers.

Someone reading the Good News Bible for the first time must have been shocked by the contrast:

> Happy are those
> who reject the advice of evil people,
> who do not follow the example of sinners
> or join those who have no use for God.

The changes are so drastic that one needs to do a check to make sure that this is really the opening verse of Psalm 1.

The first shock to the system is the replacement of the word *blessed* with the word *happy*. The word *blessed* is one of the evocative words of the traditional English Bible, and for that very reason it is on the "hit list" of a colloquial translation philosophy. The word *blessed* is the essential feature of the literary form known as the beatitude ("the state or quality of being blessed"). Whenever the word *blessed* appears in a beatitude, it is understood as actually conferring that quality, in addition to being a prayer or wish that a person be blessed. Compared to the *gravitas* of the word *blessed*, the word *happy* is a trivializing term, replacing the spiritual connotations of *blessed* with an affective, "feel good" word. We can see right here one quality of the new Bibles: a reduction of the richness of traditional translations to a mundane, one-dimensional level.

---

Whereas translators in the King James tradition have always wanted to be seen as claiming a lineage with the KJV even while creating a new translation, adherents of the new philosophy regularly distance themselves from the KJV or pay their disrespects to it in a ritual slaying of the father figure. Here are specimens:

- A modern translation needs "not to be intimidated by the King James Version peering over its shoulder."—Calvin Linton, NIV committee member
- "As long as all people had the King James Version, they didn't think." —Eugene Nida
- "Do not give them a loaf of bread, covered with an inedible, impenetrable crust, fossilized by three and half centuries."—Edwin H. Palmer, committee member of the NIV, commenting on the King James Version

---

The second shock in the GNB rendition of Psalm 1:1 is that the metaphors of the original have been removed from sight. This is as startling as reading Shakespeare or Milton with the metaphors removed. In the GNB, we find no walking down a path, no standing with a congregated group of people, no sitting in the gate (the ancient equivalent of serving on the town council).

What we get instead in each line is one possible meaning out of multiple legitimate meanings embodied in the metaphors of the original text. The GNB translators decided that one meaning that can be construed from the original metaphor of walking down a path is the idea of following someone's advice. The translators similarly decided that the poet's metaphor of standing in an assembly can mean following someone's example. And they decided that not sitting in the seat of scoffers can be interpreted as meaning not joining "those who have no use for God."

If we analyze those translation decisions, it is pretty easy to see what the new translation philosophy represented (and still represents). All of the interpretations of the original poet's metaphors are defensible, but (a) they are often not the best option for the primary meanings of the metaphors, and (b) they in any case are only one of several meanings embodied in the original metaphors. In other words, the effect of the translation maneuvers is reductionistic. Second, the aim is to be contemporary and colloquial, and this, too, can carry a price tag. To speak of someone who "has no use for God" is catchy on a first hearing, but if we try to get a precise theological meaning from the saying, we falter.

## Summary: Contrasting Styles

The foregoing comparison between the translations based on traditional and innovative translation philosophies captures in microcosm the essential nature of the seismic shift that occurred in the middle of the last century. We do not need to conduct a scholarly exploration of dynamic equivalence as a translation philosophy in order to sense the difference. We can hear the difference immediately.

## The Philosophy behind the Change

The energy that Eugene Nida and his associates brought to the task of Bible translation was breathtaking. The philosophy that underlay the new translations was thoroughly thought out, and it was explained and argued in numerous books, introductions, and essays. The main tenets were as follows.

### Slanting a Translation toward a Specific Audience

If we consult the prefaces to translations in the King James tradition, we will find no references to the concept of a target audience. We can infer that all translators up to the middle of the twentieth century had in mind a generic readership encompassing the entire range of age and ability, with no specific concessions made to any class of readers. We catch a hint of this when the preface to the KJV simply addresses the "good Christian reader."

One of the new ingredients represented by dynamic equivalent translations was a preoccupation (sometimes an obsession) with a target audience. I noted above that the GNB removed the metaphors from Psalm 1:1; in his book subtitled "How to Use the Good News Bible," Eugene Nida explained why the translators had done this. The explanation is stated casually, but it is really a bombshell if we analyze its implications. The metaphors in the opening verse of Psalm 1 were dropped because they are "not understood" and "[seem] strange . . . to many people."[1] Because Nida's viewpoint became axiomatic with dynamic equivalent translations, many people do not pause to analyze how far-reaching the results are. The following principles are implied by Nida's statement:

- Modern readers, not biblical authors, are the ones who should determine how the Bible is translated.
- Bible translators actually know what a reader can or cannot understand; they are virtually omniscient.
- Modern readers can be assumed to have minimal reading abilities, and a Bible translation should accommodate lower rather than higher reading levels.
- Further, readers can be assumed to be incapable of being educated beyond their current low reading ability.
- Bible translators are the ones who know best what a Bible reader needs to be given from the original text of the Bible,

and they should accordingly dole out what they deem best for a reader to receive, based on their presuppositions regarding a Bible reader's aptitude.

• The Bible as given contains much that is beyond modern readers to understand readily; accordingly, translators need to correct the Bible as given. In fact, modern translators can sometimes do a better job of communicating the Bible's message than the authors of the Bible did.

That is a long list, but in my view it is all embodied in Nida's cursory comment that the metaphors of Psalm 1:1 should be eliminated from an English translation because they are "not understood" and seem "strange" to "many people."

### Demotion of the Words of the Original Text

In addition to a new orientation toward target audiences, the new translation philosophy was undergirded by a devotion to linguistics as a discipline and to specific strands of thought within linguistics. The general tendency of this linguistic orientation was to demote the importance of the words that the biblical authors wrote.

An awareness of building on a different foundation from the mainstream tradition produced a dialectical mind-set among dynamic equivalent advocates in which they customarily phrase their preferences in terms of a contrast to the established tradition ("a" as opposed to "b"). The italicized phrases in the following quotations show this mind-set (italics added): "accuracy concerns the meaning of the text *rather than its form*" (Gordon Fee and Mark Strauss); central to dynamic equivalence theory is "the principle of translating meaning *in preference to form*" (Cyrus Abdi); "translating must aim primarily at . . . the reproduction of the message *rather than the conservation of the form of the utterance*" (Eugene Nida and Charles Taber). In all of these instances, the traditional translation philosophy would say "a" *by means of* "b," not *instead of* "b"—meaning *by means of* form.

When an interviewer asked Eugene Nida, "What units of written texts carry the most meaning?" Nida replied, "The phrase."[2] When pressed on the issue of whether it is difficult to give the meaning rather than the words of the original, Nida gave vent to his scorn for translators who stick with the words of the original: "This 'word worship' helps people to have confidence, but they don't understand the text. And as long as they worship words, instead of worshipping God as revealed in Jesus Christ, they feel safe."[3]

A related cornerstone of dynamic equivalent translation is the linguistic theory that meaning is something that exists apart from the actual words of the original text. This distinction appears in each of the following representative statements:

- "I decided that we've got to approach the Scripture as though it is the message and try to give its meaning, not just to repeat the words."[4]
- "The forms [of the Bible] are simply a 'vehicle' with which to get the message across to the recipients."[5]
- "*Meaning* not *form* is the goal of Bible translation."[6]

From the beginning, the goal of Bible translation has always been to capture the meaning of the Bible in the English language. What was new with the dynamic equivalent movement was the assumption that the meaning can be translated without preserving the form and words of the original.

The statements quoted above set the *meaning* of the original text *over against* the *words* of the text. This is also true of Strauss's formula "meaning-based translation,"[7] with its implication that we can get to the meaning without the words of the original text. Traditional translation had always operated on the premise of "meaning through form"; the new philosophy claimed "meaning not form."

### How Did the Paradigm Shift Happen?

I have shown that the new translation philosophy was based on a well-thought-out set of principles and, second, that these deviated from the mainstream of English Bible translation. In view of this, my observation at the start of this chapter—that paradigm shifts often occur for no better reason than that the consensus of opinion suddenly shifts—may seem incorrect. But I am talking about the process by which the new translation swept the field.

Most churches and individuals who adopted the NIV when it appeared did not do so because the principles underlying it were stated and defended in open debate. The NIV cornered the market because (a) it was the only viable alternative to the obsolete King James Bible, and (b) marketing and advertising made it irresistibly attractive to the masses. Only with the current clamoring for a more literal translation have most English Bible readers been clued in to what happened half a century ago.

The dynamic equivalent movement had a free ride for half a century. There are many signposts that the free ride is now over, and that a better-informed Bible-reading public knows what it wants in a translation, regardless of what that preference is. This has been a great gain for all Bible readers: it is important to know what we hold in our hands when we hold an English Bible.

I need to emphasize that the subject of this book is English Bible translation, not Bible translation into the language of a non-Western culture, and not into a new language that has just been codified. The problems of some aspects of the Bible in such situations are well attested. Even after we make allowance for exaggerated claims of the difficulties, no one can read about the translation issues in translations intended for non-Western cultures without seeing a certain logic to dynamic equivalence.

But translation into English is different from translation for a non-Western culture, and for me the tragedy of English Bible translation in the middle of the twentieth century stemmed from the unquestioned assumption that what was best for newly emergent languages in non-Western cultures was also best for English Bible translation. That assumption should never have been made. The English Bible is so familiar to English-speaking readers that it is virtually a native book.

Dynamic equivalent theorists usually choose illustrations from non-Western situations, confirming that translation into English does not pose the same difficulties. For example, dynamic equivalent proponents love to cite the example of cultures for which sheep are an undesirable animal (and perhaps for which goats are desirable). Well, anyone with a smattering of acquaintance with English and American literature knows about the pastoral tradition and its idealization of shepherds and sheep.

### Summary: The Philosophy behind the Change

Something entirely new entered the English Bible translation scene in the middle of the twentieth century. The principles underlying the change and the methodology based on those principles will constitute much of the content of the rest of this book, but the brief glimpse into those principles and practices given above are a good introduction to the field.

The mere fact that dynamic equivalence deviated from the historic practice of translation does not make it automatically wrong. I have noticed, however, that many dynamic equivalent proponents latch onto every shred of free translation in the history of translation as somehow validating dynamic equivalence. Apparently, therefore, historic precedence does count for something. If so, I need to reassert the main point of the three chapters that have made up Part Two of this book, namely, that until the middle of the twentieth century, English Bible translation consisted almost entirely of what came to be called "essentially literal" translation.

_____

# The Two Main Genres
# of Modern English Bible Translation

Part Three of this book explores the current English Bible translation scene in terms of a basic division that translators themselves acknowledge. "There are two general theories or methods of Bible translation," begins the preface to the New Living Translation. "There are two different approaches to translating," writes Eugene Glassman in his book *The Translation Debate*.

It should not be objectionable, therefore, that I have arranged Part Three around opposed dichotomies. Advocates of dynamic equivalence sometimes manipulate the data to make it appear that all translations are really dynamic equivalent translations. They are not. Even if we agree that all versions of the Bible can be plotted on a single continuum, the fact remains that a great divide exists in the middle of the continuum.

# 6

# DIVERGENT GOALS FOR BIBLE

# TRANSLATION

MANY BIBLE READERS are only vaguely aware that behind any translation of the Bible lies a set of goals that translators have in their minds as they sit around the committee table. Though usually hidden from view, and perhaps absent from the consciousness of a translation committee part of the time, these goals nonetheless explain a great deal about any translation of the Bible. The best way to uncover these goals is to look closely at the prefaces of Bible translations, as well as comments made by the translators if these are available.

### Common Ground

Before I highlight the divergent goals of the two main types of translation, it is important that I celebrate what all translations have in common. The disagreements between the two main genres of Bible translation are so acute, and the current debate so fervent, that it would be possible and unfortunate to allow the shared goals to drop from sight.

## Advancement of the Gospel

The first agreed-upon goal is that the purpose of Bible translation is to advance the Christian faith and bring people to saving faith in Christ. This may be a little surprising when we consider translations produced by scholars who are known to have held liberal theological views. For example, it seems likely that the word *propitiation* was dropped from the RSV because some of the translators did not believe that God was wrathful with anyone in such a way that would require an appeasing sacrifice.

Yet the concluding paragraph of the prefaces of virtually all English translations is a moving statement of how the translators hope that their translation will lead readers to embrace the message of the Bible. In fact, reading these concluding paragraphs is an excellent devotional exercise. This evangelical goal for translation as articulated in prefaces begins with William Tyndale's New Testament. Anyone who goes to Tyndale's preface expecting to find a statement of Tyndale's philosophy of translation will be disappointed. What Tyndale gives us is an outline of evangelical theology and a statement of hope that the reader will embrace the Christian gospel.

> To give the flavor of what we find in the concluding paragraph of English Bible prefaces, here are a few sentences from the preface to the RSV: "The Bible is more than a historical document to be preserved. . . . It is a record of God's dealing with men, of God's revelation of Himself and His will. It records the life and work of Him in whom the Word of God became flesh and dwelt among men. The Bible carries its full message . . . to those who read it that they may discern and understand God's Word to men."

## Clarity

A second shared goal of English Bible translators is clarity. The goal of translating the Bible, modern translators agree, is to express the content of the Bible in a manner that English-speaking readers will find clear. While this was an unstated goal from Tyndale onward, we need to credit the dynamic equivalent movement for putting clarity aggressively on the agenda of stated goals for translation.

It is not hard to see why dynamic equivalence gave clarity a high priority. Translators in the dynamic equivalent movement were motivated by the desire to produce an English text that would be easily comprehensible. Accordingly, the vocabulary of clarity became highlighted in their statements of goals. One of the stated goals of the NIV translators is that their translation "would have clarity." "Clarity and readability" are highlighted as goals of the New Living Translation, while the foreword to the Good News Bible tells us that the "new translation" seeks to convey the meaning of the Bible "clearly and accurately."

Statements like these functioned as a wake-up call to translators in the essentially literal camp. The following statements from prefaces to essentially literal translations could as well have come from dynamic equivalent translations:

- ". . . to ensure the fullest accuracy and clarity." (ESV)
- ". . . an English text that is both accurate and readable." (NKJV)
- ". . . a clear and accurate rendering of divinely-revealed truth." (NASB)

### Summary: Common Ground

For all their differences, translators in the rival camps share the goals of gospel witness and clarity of expression in the English language. These shared goals are too important to be allowed to disappear in the heat of debate.

### Divergent Goals

In the actual practice of translating, the points on which the two genres of translation *disagree* count for more than do the shared goals noted above. Ideas have consequences, and the English translations that the two philosophies produce are very different from each other because the philosophies on which they are based differ from each other.

71

## Opposing Versions of Transparency

The goal of producing a transparent text surfaced early in the dynamic equivalent movement. English Bibles in the traditional mode have always been relatively difficult books to understand. The daily newspaper is easier to read than the Bible, and it was a goal of the new translations to sound like the daily newspaper. Billy Graham praised *The Living Letters* paraphrase of Paul's epistles by saying that "it is thrilling to read the Word . . . [in] a style that reads much like today's newspaper."[1]

The goal of being immediately understandable naturally produced the concept of a *transparent text*. What this meant to dynamic equivalent translators was transparency to the modern reader. The goal was that an English translation would not call attention to itself as being different from everyday discourse and, further, that the text would be easily and immediately understood by a modern reader with modest reading abilities. The formula used in the preface to the Good News Bible is especially well known: "Every effort has been made to use language that is natural, clear, simple, and unambiguous." Literary scholar Stephen Prickett attached the label "the transparent text" to the stated goal of the Good News Bible committee.[2]

Although the *concept* of a text that is transparent to the modern reader was implicit in the stated goals of dynamic equivalent translators, the *label* "transparent text" was popularized in an essay by Stephen Prickett. As implied by the title of Prickett's essay "The Problem of the Transparent Text," Prickett took a dim view of translations that seek to be immediately grasped by a modern reader: readers who are given a transparent text "see least," Prickett wrote, while those who wrestle with the difficulties of the original text "discover most. For the former, the text has become evermore transparent—revealing nothing behind; for the latter, the text's apparent opacity has become evermore richly revealing."

Probably because the dynamic equivalent movement had made the vocabulary of the transparent text a "household phrase" among translators, adherents of the verbal-equivalence translation philosophy contemplated how the concept of transparency applies to an essentially literal philosophy of translation. Obviously a very different concept of transparency prevails with essentially literal translations.

The preface to the English Standard Version states the alternate concept of transparency when it claims that the translation "seeks to be transparent to the original text." This is a revolutionary concept of transparency compared to the dynamic equivalent use of the word *transparent*. In both versions of the concept, transparency means that all obstacles or obstructions have been removed from sight. To produce a translation that is transparent to the modern reader requires translators to remove anything that would get in the way of a reader's immediately understanding every statement that appears in the English translation.

When a translation seeks to be transparent to the original text, by contrast, the goal is to remove anything that would obstruct a reader's seeing what the original Hebrew and Greek text says. The focus of the translator's attention here is not the reader but the original text. The question then arises, what things make up the phenomenon of "what is in the original text"?

The original text is obviously made up of specific words, so transparency to that text begins at the lexical level of making sure that an English reader knows what the words of the original are. Related to that, much of the original text is poetic and figurative in expression; accordingly, taking a modern reader straight to the original text requires retaining the images and figurative language of the Bible. Third, the text of the Bible is rooted in an ancient world—a world of customs, attitudes, and prevailing ideas (a mental picture of the world, or worldview). To be transparent to the original text means preserving all signposts to the ancient world of the biblical writers, as opposed to finding equivalents to the details that make up that world. It means preserving a reference to the ancient practice of putting oil on one's head as a sign of joy (Eccl. 9:8), instead of offering the modern equivalent "a dash of cologne" (NLT).

## Allegiance to Audience versus Allegiance to Author

Another disagreement regarding the goals of translation is captured in the title of an essay on Bible translation: "To Whom Is a Translator Responsible—Reader or Author?"[3] The elevation of the reader to the role of determining how the Bible is translated entered the field with the arrival of dynamic equivalence.

As with so much in regard to modern translation theory, we can begin with Eugene Nida. One of Nida's translation principles is "the priority of the needs of the audience over the forms of language."[4] Nida then caters to readers even more specifically: "the use of language by persons twenty-five to thirty years of age has priority over the language of the older people or of children"; "in certain situations the speech of women should have priority over the speech of men."[5]

Once we know about this explicit elevation of the reader over what the text literally says, certain statements in prefaces to English translations at once fall into place. Consider the following specimens (italics added):

- ". . . to express that meaning in a manner and form easily understood *by the readers*." (GNB)
- "Metaphorical language is often difficult *for contemporary readers* to understand, so at times we have chosen to translate or illuminate the metaphor." (NLT)
- "Because *for most readers* today the phrases 'the Lord of hosts' and 'God of hosts' have little meaning, this version renders them 'the Lord Almighty' and 'God Almighty.'" (NIV)
- "Ancient customs are often unfamiliar *to modern readers*." (NCV)

Who is calling the shots here? The biblical authors and their original text? No; the modern reader is determining the translation.

It is no wonder that John MacArthur speaks slightingly—and correctly—of translations that are "more concerned with the human reader than the divine author" of the Bible.[5]

## Translating Words versus Translating Meaning

The main tradition of English Bible translation is based squarely on the principle of fidelity to the words of the original text. Until the advent of dynamic equivalence, this was mainly understood rather than stated. For the early mainstream translations, therefore, we can only *deduce* that the primary goal was to find the English words that best matched the words of the biblical text. For example, starting with the Geneva Bible, translators italicized English words that had been added to the original text. Mainly, though, we can see from the essentially literal nature of the translations that the translators accepted the principle of fidelity to the words of the original.

After the advent of dynamic equivalence, prefaces make their claims explicit in regard to the words versus meaning debate. The preface to the New King James Version contrasts its translation philosophy to dynamic equivalence with the "principle of complete equivalence [that] seeks to preserve *all* of the information in the [original] text." The ESV translators aimed "to capture the precise wording of the original text and the personal style of each Bible writer."

The first wave of dynamic equivalent translations simply omitted any statement about preserving the words of the original and instead spoke of translating the meaning of the original. For a public uninitiated into the changes that had entered the translation scene, there was no way of knowing how drastically the translation that they held in their hands had altered the rules of the game. Here is a sampling of statements, with the key phrases italicized to highlight the kernel of each statement:

- "The first concern of the translators has been . . . fidelity *to the thought* of the biblical writers." (NIV)

- The translator's "first task was to understand correctly *the meaning* of the original." (GNB)
- ". . . to reclothe *the meaning* of the original in the words and structure of American English." (SEB)
- "Every attempt has been made to produce a text that is faithful to *the meaning* of the original." (CEV)

None of these prefaces clarifies that the translators' primary devotion to the "thought" or "meaning" of the Bible is *in place of* primary devotion to the words of the original.

More recent dynamic equivalent prefaces have done a better job of informing their readers exactly what the goal of the translators has been. The preface to the New Living Translation is exemplary in this regard. It clearly describes the two rival translation philosophies and then stakes its claim with dynamic equivalence: "A thought-for-thought translation . . . has the potential to represent the intended meaning of the original text even more accurately than a word-for-word translation." Additionally, even though most dynamic equivalent prefaces do not clarify the rejection of fidelity to the words of the original, proponents often have done so elsewhere, as with Eugene Nida's comment in an interview. When asked what he considered his most important contribution to Bible translation, Nida repied, "To help people . . . say what the text means—*not what the words are*, but what the text means" (italics added).[6]

**What Is at Stake in the Words versus Meaning Debate**

What is at stake in the disagreement about whether a translation should give a reader the corresponding English words and phrases for what the original text contains, or whether translators should give only their understanding of the ideas ("meaning") of the original text? Two things at least.

First, dynamic equivalence regularly *substitutes* something in place of the original text. Instead of saying that "the almond tree blossoms" (Eccl. 12:5), as all essentially literal translations render it, a dynamic equivalent translation reads "your hair will turn white" (GNB). In the second translation, the reader has no way of knowing that the original text contains the image of a blossoming almond tree. When that maneuver is spread out over the entire Bible, the reader ends up with a substitute for what the biblical authors wrote. What is at stake, therefore, is whether a reader will have the actual Bible in English, or a "virtual" Bible at one or two removes from the original.

Second, the very concept of language and communication is contested in the divergent philosophies of translation. Dynamic equivalent theorists regularly assert that meaning exists independent of words. They claim that translators can give the meaning of the original biblical text without retaining the words. Gordon Fee and Mark Strauss, for example, write that "accuracy concerns the *meaning* of the text rather than its form."[7] "Rather than its form"—that is at the heart of the difference between the rival translation philosophies.

> Experts in literature and communication theory regularly assert that meaning gets communicated *through form*, starting with the very words of an utterance but extending to genres such as story or metaphor. Ideas and meaning do not exist apart from the words and genres in which they are embodied. Here are three famous statements of the principle:
>
> - "Form is meaning."—Literary critic Cleanth Brooks
> - "The medium is the message."—Communication theorist Marshall McCluhan
> - "One does not make poetry with ideas but with *words*."—French poet Mallarmé, in reply to a poet who lamented his inability to write poetry even though he was "full of ideas."

Eugene Nida provided an interesting twist on this issue when he answered the question, "What units of written texts carry the most meaning?" Nida replied, "The phrase."[8] It is of course true that words by themselves do not convey a speaker's meaning. It is the arrangement of the words into sentences that communicate meaning. But of what do phrases and sentences consist? They consist of words.

Proponents of an essentially literal translation philosophy do not see how meaning can exist without form. In the words of Jack Collins, "Without form, you lose meaning."[9] For translators in the "essentially literal" camp, what is at stake is clear and logical thinking about the nature of language and communication.

## Summary: Divergent Goals

Although translators generally agree on the goals of gospel witness and clarity of communication, other goals turn out to have more impact on the actual process of translation than those two points of agreement. The differences between transparency to a modern reader versus transparency to the original text, between allegiance to biblical authors versus allegiance to modern readers, and between translation of words versus feeling free to abandon the words of the original are not simply differences of degree. The difference between essentially literal translation and dynamic equivalence is "not one of degree but of kind."[10]

# 7

# DIVERGENT VIEWS OF THE BIBLE

IS IT REALLY POSSIBLE that proponents of the rival translation philosophies have divergent views of the Bible? I can imagine that some of my readers will find this suggestion inherently unlikely. The differing views of the Bible are not something that translators themselves are likely to assert. We therefore need to *infer* the conception of the Bible that translators hold in their minds as they translate. This partly involves teasing out the inferences of statements that we find in the prefaces to English Bibles, as well as in books and articles that the translators have written.

In this chapter I will mainly operate at a level of generalization about differing views of the Bible. Later chapters will provide illustrations of my generalizations.

## Is the Bible an Ancient or Modern Book?
I begin with a dichotomy that is obvious and that I trust will gain initial credibility for my claim of divergent views of the Bible. Whereas the practices of essentially literal translators are an implied acknowledgment that the Bible is an ancient book, dynamic equivalent translators consistently chart their compass in a contrary direction.

## Modernizing the Biblical Text

It is true that dynamic equivalent proponents do not state outright that the Bible is a modern book. But when we look closely at their theoretic statements about translation, we can see a bias in the direction of claiming that details that make the Bible appear to be an ancient rather than modern book are a blemish or misrepresentation that needs to be corrected or removed from sight. By the time these translators remove the alleged blemishes, therefore, the Bible reads largely like a modern book. Several avenues confirm the picture I have just sketched.

We can profitably start with representative statements in the prefaces to dynamic equivalent translations. Here are three specimen statements:

- "Ancient customs are often unfamiliar to modern readers. . . . So these are clarified either in the text or in a footnote." (NCV)
- "This version of the New Testament in a contemporary idiom keeps the language of the Message current and fresh and understandable in the same language in which we do our shopping, talk with our friends, worry about world affairs, and teach our children their table manners." (MESSAGE)
- "We have sought to translate terms shrouded in history or culture in ways that can be immediately understood by the contemporary reader." (NLT)

The key words in those quotations are *modern* and *contemporary*. Furthermore, the point of agreement among these sources is that the Bible should be translated in such a way as to seem familiar rather than unfamiliar to modern readers. A book that seems familiar to a modern reader is a modern book.

One dimension of this modernity is the style into which the Bible is cast during the process of translation. In an earlier chapter I noted Billy Graham's endorsement of *The Living Letters* paraphrase of the epistles as possessing "a style that reads much like today's newspaper."[1] A book that reads like the daily newspaper cannot possibly avoid seeming like a modern book to its readers.

This is reinforced by the formula that dynamic equivalent translators regularly invoke, namely, that the Bible should be translated in such a way that it reads "as we would say it." Or, to state it the other way, dynamic equivalent translators reject renditions about which it can be said that "no one speaking English in the real world would use an expression like [that]."[2] Eugene Peterson is said to have translated Paul's letters in keeping with his mental question, "If Paul were the pastor of my church, how would he say this?"[3]

In addition to translating into a prevailingly modern style, dynamic equivalent translators sometimes remove references to ancient customs and the ancient mind-set of biblical writers. This, too, is a way of giving Bible readers a modern Bible. For example, Paul's command to "greet one another with a holy kiss" (1 Cor. 16:20) becomes "shake hands all round as a sign of Christian love" (PHILLIPS).

### The Bible as an Ancient Book

By contrast, essentially literal translations begin with the premise that the Bible is an ancient book, far removed from modern Western readers in time, geography, and customs. In its original form, these signposts exist on nearly every page. That is not open to dispute. The contested point is whether the signposts should be dimmed or removed in the process of translation. For multiple reasons, essentially literal translators believe that the ancientness of the biblical text should be preserved.

The first reason they adduce is accuracy. The Bible is literally an ancient rather than modern book. To transform it into a modern book is to cut against the grain and create a false impression for readers. Part of that false impression is that the Bible is removed from real, space-time history, being situated instead in a floating "ahistorical" world. The realm of imaginative literature can help us see that this is an untenable approach. The whole effect of Chaucer's *Canterbury Tales* would be lost if a translator camouflaged that the Canterbury pilgrims rode on horses rather than in cars, that they stayed in inns rather than motels, and that they contended with mire on the roads instead of traffic jams.

---

- "It is . . . not in the translator's province to lift the Bible out of its milieu. He should not try to dehistoricize it, reset it, or deculturize it. God chose to give His revelation in history at certain times and places."—John H. Skilton
- "God has revealed himself to men in space-time history—to particular men and women, spatially and temporally and linguistically located. If we are not very cautious [in changing] the historical particulars, we may introduce such substantive anachronisms that the story becomes intrinsically unbelievable."—D. A. Carson

---

Second, advocates of essentially literal translation believe that when translators remove the original world from sight they take away readers' opportunity to confront the Bible as something "other" than their own familiar assumptions. The Bible should potentially challenge rather than immediately confirm familiar ways of viewing reality. As biblical scholar Raymond Van Leeuwen puts it, "We need a translation that allows the Bible to say what it says, even if that seems strange and odd to readers at first glance. If God is 'other' than we are, we should be willing to work at the 'otherness' of the Bible, in order to understand what the Lord is saying through his Word."[4]

Individual modernizing touches might seem innocuous, but the cumulative effect is drastic. To make Psalm 84:10 read "the homes of the wicked" (CEV) rather than "the tents of wickedness" (ESV) might seem like a small matter, but when spread over the entire Bible, such adjustments conceal the world of the text, with its potential to challenge modern ways of viewing the world, and replace it with a familiar suburban world that finally misleads a reader.

## Is the Bible a Simple Book?

Translators in the two camps also disagree about whether the Bible is a simple or difficult book. Here, too, we need to "read between the lines" to tease out the implications of what prefaces and translators say about the respective translations.

### The Bible as a Simple Book

Sometimes dynamic equivalent proponents come right out and declare that the Bible is a simple book. But even when they do not, their preoccupation with translating the Bible into a form that is immediately understood by unsophisticated readers projects the image of a simple book (with the resulting translations ensuring that it is received as such by readers). Here are specimen statements by dynamic equivalent advocates:

- Since God "stooped to the level of human language to communicate with his people," the translators' task is to set forth the "truth of the biblical revelation in language that is as clear and simple as possible."[5]
- "Jesus talked plainly to people. . . . Jesus, the master Teacher, was very careful not to give people more than they could grasp. . . . We are trying to re-capture that level of communication. . . . Jesus was able to communicate clearly, even with children." (SEB)
- "After ascertaining as accurately as possible the meaning of the original, the translators' next task was to express that meaning in a manner and form easily understood by the readers." (GNB)

The key concepts here are *simple, plain,* and *easily.*

We will observe the effects of this philosophy in later chapters, but here it is enough to note that if translation committees begin with the assumption of wishing to deliver a simple Bible, their actual translation will match that conception. Vocabulary and syntax will be simple. Readers will receive help with figurative language, either by removal or with accompanying commentary.

Theological language may be eliminated, and rhetorical patterning will often be obscured.

I need to pause to note a paradox regarding the dynamic equivalent viewpoint. Although (as noted above) the vocabulary with which dynamic equivalent translators describe the Bible stresses that it is a simple book for the common person, when these translators talk about the corrections and adjustments that need to be made for modern readers (e.g., figurative language removed or interpreted), they implicitly acknowledge that in its original form the Bible has much about it that is difficult. But in turn the whole bent of these translators is toward removing the difficulties en route to producing a simple, readily understood English Bible.

## The Contrasting View of the Bible

The contrasting view of the Bible cannot be reduced to a single formula. The opposite of simple might be *complex*, or it might be *difficult*, or it might be *varied* (in contrast to the uniformly simple style of an easy-reading translation in which the governing principle throughout is to render the Bible at a grade-school or junior-high reading level).

> "One cannot escape the fact that the Bible contains many concepts and expressions which are difficult for the modern reader. There is no evidence that they were much less so for the original readers. They, too, had to cope with technical terminology, with thousands of OT allusions and with Hebrew loan words, idioms and translation that must have been very strange to many of them."—Anthony Howard Nichols

One of the statements quoted above based its argument on the discourse methods of Jesus, and this is a good starting point here. Jesus himself gave this explanation of why he spoke in parables: "To you [the disciples] it has been given to know . . . but to them [the unbelieving masses] it has not been given. . . . This is why I speak to them in parables, because seeing they do not see, and hearing they do not hear, nor do they understand" (Matt. 13:11, 13, ESV).

This is a very mysterious statement, already giving the lie to the claim that Jesus' statements are simple and easy to understand. I interpret Jesus' explanation of his parabolic method to mean that he did not intend his statements to carry all of their meaning on the surface. We might infer that Jesus' discourse method involves delayed-action insight: those who ponder Jesus' sayings will come to understand them, whereas people who are unwilling to penetrate beneath the surface will not.

Is the Bible a simple book? On balance it is a difficult book, filled with mysterious statements (including poetic statements) that require analysis, unpacking, and not infrequently research before we understand them. I believe that nearly any ten-minute reading from the Bible will present much that is baffling and difficult and, further, that such a reading will virtually never present material that carries all its meaning on the surface.

## Does the Bible Need to Be Corrected?

A third area of disagreement between dynamic equivalent translations and essentially literal ones focuses on whether the Bible is a deficient book that needs to be corrected, at least for a modern reader. I have no doubt that dynamic equivalent translators will deny that they believe that the Bible in its original form is deficient. But their statements reveal otherwise. We can begin with the following statements:

- "It was recognised that it was often appropriate to mute the patriarchalism of the culture of the biblical writers." (NIVI)

- "Metaphorical language is often difficult for contemporary readers to understand, so at times we have chosen to translate or illuminate the metaphor." (NLT)

- "In everyday speech, 'gender generic' or 'inclusive' language is used, because it sounds most natural to people today. This means that where the biblical languages require

85

masculine nouns or pronouns when both men and women are intended, this intention must be reflected in translation, though the English *form* may be very different from that of the original." (CEV)

- "Sentences are purposely kept short, transparent, and uncomplicated to promote greater understanding. Complex sentence structures are often unnecessary anyway." (SEB)
- "The unsophisticated" reader "is likely to be grateful . . . at being delivered from theological subtleties" in this translation.[6]
- This translation "*breathes new life* into the enduring wisdom of the ancient biblical texts." (dust jacket of *The Message*; italics added to highlight the implication that the Bible needs resuscitation)

Despite a range of motivations in these statements, all of them have something in common: they begin with the premise that there are things about the Bible that need to be changed for the contemporary reader. Further, the translations based on these principles do, in fact, change the Bible to bring it into alignment with the specific criticisms or dislikes that are voiced. In short, the translations based on these statements "correct" the Bible.

Prefaces to dynamic equivalent translations represent the Bible as a problematical book. They use phrases such as "often unfamiliar" (NCV), "often difficult" (NLT), and "have little meaning" for "most readers today" (NIV). By contrast, the preface to the Geneva Bible of 1560 did not find the Bible problematical: the Bible is "the light to our paths, the key of the kingdom of heaven, our comfort in affliction, our shield and sword against Satan, the school of all wisdom, the glass wherein we behold God's face, the testimony of his favor, and the only food and nourishment of our souls."

That translators in the "essentially literal" camp do not believe that the Bible needs to be corrected is evident from their practices. These translators do not change gender references. They do not eliminate or add interpretive commentary to figurative expressions. They retain weighty theological language. They do not find a lifeless Bible that needs to have new energy infused into it.

### Summary: Does the Bible Need to Be Corrected?

Bible translations always reflect how a translator or committee views the Bible. Although virtually all prefaces to English Bibles signal the committees' acceptance of the authority of the Bible and (if done by evangelical believers) its inspiration, those claims should not be allowed to obscure irreconcilable differences in viewpoint between the Bible as an ancient versus modern book, as a simple versus complex/difficult book, and as a book that does or does not need to be corrected for a modern reader.

# 8

# DIVERGENT VIEWS
# OF THE BIBLE'S AUTHORS,
# READERS, AND TRANSLATORS

WITH THE THREE TOPICS that I cover in this chapter, I have in each case started with dynamic equivalence. Advocates of that approach have made the most visible statements about the authors, readers, and translators of the Bible. The essentially literal position has been largely implied rather than stated overtly.[1]

## The Authors of the Bible

There is no scarcity of evidence that the Bible is in eclipse in the evangelical world. Expository preaching based on a close reading of a biblical passage is nearly extinct in evangelical pulpits. In contrast to what prevailed fifteen years ago, virtually no young people entering college today claim to have had a high-school church experience that included small-group Bible studies. Teaching the Bible was once a hot topic at the annual meeting of college professors of Christian education, but today it is a subject of neglect.

## Diminished Respect for Biblical Authors

I myself see parallels between the situation I have described and trends in modern Bible translation. One of the parallels is diminished respect for the authors of the Bible. One of the formulas that I hear most often is the one that speaks of "what Paul *was trying to say* in this passage." Similarly, one of the most common inductive Bible study questions in my circles is, what is the author *trying to say* in this passage?

People who use the formula do not intend to disparage the writers of the Bible. They are simply repeating what has become a cliché. The cliché does, however, signal a loss of respect for biblical authors. The "trying to say" formula implies that the writers of the Bible were either inept in expressing themselves clearly or that they lacked the resources to say what they were thinking.

It is no surprise that this syndrome has become so common. The attitude is right there in the prefaces to some modern English Bible translations. The preface to the NIV claims that the phrases *Lord of hosts* and *God of hosts* "have little meaning" for "most readers today." "Where there was potential for confusion," states the New Century Bible, "rhetorical questions have been stated according to their implied answer," signaling that the presence of rhetorical questions in the Bible invites confusion. Another preface states that the translation has eliminated "religious words" such as *church, justification,* and *redemption* to match the reading level of modern readers (SEB).

Surely there is no intention to discredit the competence of the writers of the Bible. But we need to analyze the impression of the Bible that a reader carries away from statements like the ones I quoted. Steady exposure to such statements gradually creates skepticism about the adequacy of the Bible as it was originally written. Readers are smart enough to ask who is responsible for the difficulties that the Bible allegedly possesses. The biblical *authors* are obviously the ones responsible for the Bible as we have it. Today, Bible readers often betray a lack of confidence that the writers of the Bible *said* thus and so and instead perceive the writers as *trying to say* it.

> How we speak of the biblical text quickly becomes an implied statement about how we view the writers of the Bible. The following comment by a literary critic evokes a very different picture of biblical writers than do the prefaces of some modern Bible translations: "I hold up a picture of the author of Ruth as an artist in full command of a complex and subtle art, which art is exhibited in almost every word of the story." —D. H. Rauber

## The Implied View of Essentially Literal Translators

What about essentially literal translations? The answer is an argument from silence. Prefaces to essentially literal translations say nothing about the difficulty of the text for modern readers. The translators apparently believe that readers can rise to the level that the original text requires in such areas as figurative language, rhetorical patterns, vocabulary, and references to the ancient world of the authors.

The devotion of essentially literal translators to preserve the actual words of the Bible's writers is likewise an implicit endorsement of the ability of the writers to say what they meant. The essentially literal philosophy carries within it an inherent safeguard against the view that the authors of the Bible produced a Bible that is beset with deficiencies for a modern reader. When essentially literal translators preserve the words of the original authors, they signal their confidence that the authors used the right words.

## Bible Readers

In an earlier chapter I noted that the elevation of the reader to the status of a "major player" in the translation enterprise, even to the extent of determining how the Bible is translated, is a contribution of the dynamic equivalent movement. I will not retread that territory here. My concern rather is the specific picture of the Bible reader that dynamic equivalent translators assume as they sit around the committee table and write the prefaces to their translations.

## How Dynamic Equivalence Views Bible Readers

The overall picture that emerges from the prefaces is a reader with decidedly limited reading abilities. We can see this, for example, in what is loosely called "reading level," which depends on a combination of vocabulary and syntax. One preface speaks of limiting its vocabulary to three thousand words (SEB). Another preface claims that the translators aimed to reach "a junior high school student" (NLT). The chief translator for the Good News Bible claimed that the translation was aimed at the elementary-school reading level.[2]

Along with the assumption of a grade-school reading level we find references to the difficulty modern readers have with theological vocabulary and concepts. One preface claims that in an effort to produce a translation "that can be understood by everyone, especially by those who have never read the Bible," the translators avoided using certain traditional theological terms (SEB). Another translation is similarly committed to "avoidance of traditionally theological language and biblical words" (CEV). Prefaces like these paint a picture of a Bible reader handicapped in dealing with theological language.

There is no need to belabor this point. The prefaces to "easy reading" Bibles present a united front in regard to their assumed readers. Other sections of my book discuss further types of assumed impairment in Bible readers, and I will avoid duplication here. These additional assumptions include the inability of readers to understand figurative language and references to foreign customs in the world of the biblical text, and the need for short sentences. While leaving those topics untouched here, I nonetheless wish to draw two additional inferences.

First, the prefaces I have quoted make an assumption (never stated) that readers cannot advance beyond their current level of reading and comprehension. Readers are permanently fixed at a grade-school reading level. The irony of this is that even if readers do advance beyond a grade-school level (as all of them do), their advance will do them no good when it comes to dynamic equivalent translations, because those translations have been permanently rendered at a grade-school level.

Second, dynamic equivalent proponents overwhelmingly assert that the difficulties posed by the original biblical text are either unique to modern readers or especially acute for them. Prefaces regularly use such formulas as "to modern readers" (NCV), "by the contemporary reader" (NLT), and "most readers today" (NIV). The effect is to isolate modern readers as a "special needs" group, and the whole dynamic equivalent enterprise can be viewed as an attempt to meet the special needs of impaired modern readers.

## The Response of Essentially Literal Translators

It is possible to infer how essentially literal translators would respond to the assumptions that dynamic equivalent translators make about Bible readers, but before we tease out those inferences, we need again to note an argument from silence. The prefaces to essentially literal translations assert no presuppositions about modern Bible readers. It is a fair inference that the translators do not believe that the difficulties of the biblical text are insurmountable for educated adult readers, though surely these translators also acknowledge that any text coming to us from the ancient past contains much that requires explanation to a modern reader.

---

The following two quotations highlight the different conceptions of Bible readers held by dynamic equivalent translators and essentially literal translators, respectively:

- "Statistics released by the National Center for Education indicate that 'almost half of U.S. adults have very limited reading and writing skills.' If this is the case, a contemporary translation must be a text that an inexperienced reader can read."—Preface to CEV
- "It is better to teach each new generation the meaning of the Bible's technical terms than to eliminate them and produce a generation [of people who] are biblically and theologically illiterate from having suffered long-term exposure to inaccurate and imprecise versions of the Bible."—Robert Martin

---

The first assumption that advocates of essentially literal translation would dispute is that a grade-schooler should serve as the norm for reading ability and comprehension. In what other areas of life do we accept a grade-school level of expression and comprehension as the norm and "cap" for society as a whole? There is no sphere in which our society operates permanently at a sixth- or seventh-grade level. The preface to the New Living Translation equates "the average reader" with "a junior high student," but the equation is false: the average reader in our society is not a junior high student. Most English Bible readers have received at least some education beyond the high school level. The dynamic equivalent experiment actually expects less from Bible readers than our society expects in other areas.

A second point of dispute is the degree to which we can and should educate Bible readers as they confront the difficulties of the biblical text. The dynamic equivalent movement is a massive experiment in capitulation to low levels of reading ability and comprehension.

Proponents of essentially literal translations are unwilling to make that capitulation. Instead, they are ready to shoulder the task of educating modern readers. They stand in the line of William Tyndale, who actually added words like *intercession* and *atonement* to the English language in an attempt to transmit the content of the Bible. In the sixteenth and seventeenth centuries, Bible translation was a leading contributor to the rise of literacy in England.[3] Essentially literal translations have as an unstated motto Paul's command "do not be children in your thinking" (1 Cor. 14:20).

Finally, essentially literal translators do not generally agree with dynamic equivalent translators that modern readers constitute a special case when compared to earlier readers. This is not to say that the customs and idiomatic expressions of the ancient world do not pose difficulties. But the original readers of the Bible were not as exempt from these difficulties as some translators claim. As one writer on the subject asks rhetorically, "Did the average speaker of *koine* Greek find no difficulty in 2 Peter

2:4–9 or Romans 2:14–21? . . . Did all the congregation of the Galatian church grasp the whole of Paul's letter to them when it was first read?"[4]

In a similar vein, translator E. V. Rieu stated the view that "there is good reason for thinking that the original audience of the Gospels found them just as difficult as we do; and if therefore we paraphrase or lower our standard of English in order to make things crystal clear to the so-called man in the street, we're going beyond our jobs as translators."[5] We need to remember, too, that one of the "difficulties" that some modern translations wish to remove from the text is figurative language, and we *know* that figurative language was present in the Bible from the beginning.

### Summary: Bible Readers

The opposed views of Bible readers that the two Bible translation camps hold are one of the most unbridgeable points of disagreement. Once dynamic equivalent translators created their image of modern Bible readers as low-level readers, and then additionally when they committed themselves to slant their translation toward this assumed reader, their methods of translation were inevitable. Essentially literal translators never accepted as accurate or desirable the assumed audience of dynamic equivalent translators, and in that refusal lay an equally inevitable methodology for translation.

### Bible Translators

It would be easy to assimilate what I have said about biblical authors and readers without realizing that rival views of the translator permeate the attitudes I have surveyed. Let me begin on a positive note in regard to dynamic equivalent translators: they are extremely eager to please their readers and give them what they want. Of course there are major problems with that eagerness to please, but I want to credit dynamic equivalent translators with being allies of Bible readers as they confront the difficulties that the Bible often poses.

## How Dynamic Equivalent Translators View Their Role

I began this chapter by exploring the preoccupation of dynamic equivalent translators with the alleged difficulties that the Bible possesses. Dynamic equivalent translators implicitly view it as their role to break open the prison of misunderstanding with which the Bible continually threatens to enslave its readers. The Bible is an inherently difficult book, in this view, and the translator is a jail breaker who can free readers from the difficulties.[6]

From this view flow the roles that dynamic equivalent translators add to the simple role of translator (understood as finding the best English words by which to express the lexical meanings of the words of the original authors). One of these added roles is that of exegete or commentator. Dynamic equivalent translators often feel constrained to add explanatory material right in the translation to make sure that readers have at their disposal the translators' preferred interpretation of a word or phrase.

I wish not to exaggerate; while dynamic equivalent translators are always *ready* to add interpretive commentary to their translation, with only a minority of verses do they actually do so. The problem, however, is that with a dynamic equivalent translation a reader never knows where the process of translation ends and where the added layer of commentary begins.

If we ask why dynamic equivalent translators assume the mantle of exegete and commentator in addition to translator, the answer is that they are convinced that they have superior knowledge about the meaning of the Bible. They know more than most of their readers and are determined to make the right interpretive choices for their readers. The result is that these translators regularly make preemptive interpretive strikes without readers' even knowing that this has been done.

The differing conceptions of the translator are encapsulated in the following quotations. The first is Eugene Nida's explanation (noted earlier) of why he thinks translators should make up readers' minds for them on questions of interpretation; the second expresses an essentially literal translator's creed:
- "The average reader is usually much less capable of making correct judgments about . . . alternative meanings than is the translator, who can make use of the best scholarly judgments on ambiguous passages."
- "The translator, who is a steward of the work of another, is not called upon to revise or rewrite his original. . . . He is required to be faithful to what is before him."—John H. Skilton

Another role that dynamic equivalent translators assume is that of editor. One of the functions that an editor in a publishing house performs is massaging the style of what an author has written. In keeping with what I said above about the conception that dynamic equivalent translators have of their readers, a very discernible effect of these translators' editorial hand is the simplification of the style of the Bible, which usually entails a move toward a colloquial style. If Luke 6:24 reads, "Woe to you who are rich" (ESV), the dynamic equivalent translator dons an editor's cap and makes it read, "You rich people are in for trouble" (CEV), or, "It will be horrible for you, you rich and selfish people" (SEB).

## Metaphors for the Rival Views of the Translator

Essentially literal translators conceive of the translator's task in much more limited terms than do dynamic equivalent translators. They refuse to add anything to a translator's job description beyond the task of translating, defined as finding the English words that most accurately correspond to the words of the original. One metaphor that captures this stance is that of a steward—a servant to whom a master entrusts something. Essentially literal translators are also like the heralds of ancient Greek and Roman society who delivered a message that originated with someone above them. Heralds trusted the ability of their message to achieve

97

its effects without any changes or attempted enhancement on their part.[7]

Dynamic equivalent translators conceive of their task more like the orators of classical culture, who thought that the effectiveness of their communication rested on their ability to be winsome to their audiences. The orator was "audience- and results-driven," and his methods were governed by the need to "adapt his message to his audience in every possible way."[8] This exactly describes dynamic equivalent translators.

An additional metaphor that dynamic equivalent translators absolutely love to quote is that "the translator is always a traitor." I have yet to find an essentially literal translator apply this metaphor to his or her task. The "traitor" metaphor draws attention to the fact that sometimes no word or phrase in the receptor language captures the exact nuances of a word in the original language, with the result that the translation at some level "betrays" the original. Dynamic equivalent translators love the metaphor of the translator as traitor because if the translator is "always" a traitor, translators have license to depart from the actual words of the original whenever they wish. After all, they cannot *avoid* being a "traitor," so why not be a traitor at will?

### Summary: Bible Translators

The differing conceptions of the Bible's authors, readers, and translators are irreconcilable. People who try to put all translations on a continuum and claim that the differences are merely matters of degree need to look at how the two groups of translators line up on the three topics that I have covered in this chapter.

# 9

# Divergent Methods
# of Translation

UP TO THIS POINT I have delineated the differences between
the two kinds of translation largely on the basis of statements
made by translators, especially in prefaces to Bible translations.
The time has come to flesh out the generalizations that I have
made with examples.

## Fidelity to the Words of the Original versus Departure
## from Them

No issue is more central to the translation debate than the question of how strictly translators should give the English equivalent
or corresponding words for the words of the original. On the
essentially literal side, we find the axiom that "not just ideas, but
words are important."[1] On the dynamic equivalent side, we hear
the sentiment that a translation that departs from verbal correspondence "has the potential to represent the intended meaning
of the original text even more accurately than a word-for-word
translation" (preface to NLT). What difference does this disagree-

ment make in actual translation? A couple of comparisons will show at a glance that it makes a huge difference.

## Differing Ways of Translating Poetry

An essentially literal rendition of Psalm 139:5a is as follows (NRSV, ESV; NIV nearly identical):

> You hem me in, behind and before,
>     and lay your hand upon me.

Here is what a range of dynamic equivalent translations do with the verse:

> You are all around me on every side;
>     you protect me with your power. (GNB)

> You keep close guard behind and before me
>     and place your hand upon me. (REB)

> You both precede and follow me.
>     You place your hand of blessing on my head. (NLT)

> . . . with your powerful arm
>     you protect me
>     from every side. (CEV)

With a little analysis, we can see that the following things have happened in the dynamic equivalent translations: (1) the metaphor of being hemmed in or "enclosed" (NASB) is removed in all four translations; (2) the image of God's placing his hand on the speaker is replaced with the more abstract or conceptual vocabulary of *protect, power,* and *powerful* in two of the translations; (3) the impulse to make sure the reader gets the point by adding an interpretive layer on the straightforward statement of the original is evident in the phrase "hand *of blessing*"; (4) the traditional reading of the first line ("behind and before") is subverted by an original and quite different interpretation in the rendition "both precede and follow me"; (5) the metaphor of being hemmed in or enclosed is not simply removed but replaced by the different metaphor of "keep[ing] close guard."

With this single verse we can see the entire methodology of the two approaches highlighted. Essentially literal translations find the corresponding English words and leave it to the reader to interpret the lines correctly. Dynamic equivalent translators are not content with that. They attempt to make sure that readers will grasp the statements without interpretive effort (hence the removal of the metaphors of the original). They impose an interpretive layer on the material through abstraction or added commentary. And they sometimes challenge traditional readings of a verse.

> "It is hard to know what the Bible *means* when we are uncertain about what it *says*. , , , The problem with [functional equivalence] translations (i.e., most modern translations) is that they prevent the reader from inferring *meaning* because they change what the Bible *said*."— Raymond C. Van Leeuwen

## Differing Ways of Translating Prose

Here is a test case from the New Testament. An essentially literal translation of Matthew 6:22–23 reads thus:

> The eye is the lamp of the body. So, if your eye is healthy, your whole body will be full of light, but if your eye is bad, your whole body will be full of darkness. If then the light in you is darkness, how great is the darkness! (ESV; others, including NIV, virtually identical)

That passage embodies one strand of writing in the New Testament by virtue of its mystery and essentially metaphoric nature.

We could predict what dynamic equivalent translations will do with such a passage, and it turns out that they fulfill our expectations:

> Your eye is a lamp for your body. A pure eye lets sunshine into your soul. But an evil eye shuts out the light and plunges you

into darkness. If the light you think you have is really darkness, how deep that darkness will be! (NLT)

Your eye is like a lamp for the body. If your eye can see clearly, then the whole body is made bright. But if your eye is dark with sin, then your whole body is made dark. If the light in you becomes dark, how great is that darkness! (SEB)

Your eyes are like a window for your body. When they are good, you have all the light you need. Buy when your eyes are bad, everything is dark. If the light inside you is dark, you surely are in the dark. (CEV)

Your eyes are windows into your body. If you open your eyes wide in wonder and belief, your body fills up with light. If you live squinty-eyed in greed and distrust, your body is a dank cellar. If you pull the blinds on your windows, what a dark life you will have! (MESSAGE)

Even a cursory reading of the passages leaves us with an accurate general impression: the translators are continuously nervous about the possibility that readers will be unable to handle the passage accurately and/or easily in its untouched form. As a result, the translators have become commentators as well translators, constantly tugging at the original text to make it something different from what the original text says: "sunshine into your soul"; "plunges you into darkness"; "dark with sin"; "a window for your body"; "all the light you need"; "open your eyes wide in wonder and belief"; "pull the blinds on your windows."

### Ideas Have Consequences

Do the rival translation theories that I sketched in earlier chapters produce discernibly different translations? They do, and one of the points of difference focuses on whether the translators are committed to finding corresponding English words for the words of the original, or if they feel free to give both more and less than what the original states.

In its unchecked form, dynamic equivalence regularly removes a reader from the original text. In a dynamic equivalent translation we read this: "But as for me, I came so close to the edge of the cliff! / My feet were slipping, and I was almost gone" (Ps. 73:2, NLT). Another rendition of that verse reads, "I nearly missed it, / missed seeing [God's] goodness" (MESSAGE). The problem is that the original text says nothing about the edge of a cliff, about being almost gone, or about missing something. Dynamic equivalent translations are quite capable of giving us a substitute Bible. When that happens, a reader who operates on the premise that such a translation expresses what the original text says is in fact far removed from the Bible as God gave it.

## Verbal Correspondence versus Paraphrase

Not many English translators wish to be regarded as paraphrasing the Bible. Even the extremely free Simplified English Bible attempts to assure us in its preface that it "is not a paraphrase" (boldface in original). The Good News Bible is "[distinct] from a paraphrase," Eugene Nida claims.[2] We should not allow such statements to deter us from testing the claims.

Before we do so, however, we need to consider one of the oddest comments on record, namely, that "all translations paraphrase to one degree or another, since all change Hebrew and Greek words into English ones to make the text understandable."[3] Translation is never identical with a text in its original language; if it were, it would not be a translation. But within that parameter, we need terminology to differentiate translations that limit their renditions to English words that correspond to the words of the original text from those that add to and subtract from those words. The concept of paraphrase is a useful term by which to make that differentiation.

### Defining Paraphrase

In common parlance, to paraphrase means "to put into your own words." Even that description is not true of essentially literal translations, for the following reason. When we use the formula "put into our own words," we imply changing the original statement in discernible ways, usually in an attempt to clarify. The word *paraphrase* is based on the root words *para*, meaning "beside" or "beyond," and *phrazein*, meaning "to explain" or "to tell." Dictionary definitions thus define the word as meaning "to recast, rephrase, or reword, often to clarify meaning," or "to restate using other words," or "to restate a text or passage in another form or with other words." It is of course true that to translate requires one to restate or recast a statement in different words (the words of another language). But that is a metaphoric or very specialized use of the word *paraphrase*.

> "My notion of effective translation of the Bible involves a high degree of literalism—within the limits of reasonably acceptable literary English—both in regard to representing the word choices and the word order of the Hebrew. . . . The precedent of the King James Version has played a decisive and constructive role in directing readers of English to a rather literal experience of the Bible, and . . . this precedent can be ignored only at considerable cost, as nearly all the English versions of the Bible done in recent decades show." —Literary critic Robert Alter
>
> "To translate meaning while ignoring the way that meaning has been articulated is not translation at all but merely replacement—murdering the original instead of recreating it." —Gerald Hammond

Most aspects of the definitions quoted above apply to dynamic equivalent translations only. Dynamic equivalent translators often go "beyond" what the original authors said. They "explain beyond" what the original text states. They reword (not simply translate) in such a way as to clarify beyond what the biblical authors expressed.

### Paraphrase in Practice

But "the proof is in the pudding," so we should turn to actual examples. Surely we would all agree that hymn paraphrases of the psalms are a standard for what we mean by paraphrase. Here is part of George Herbert's paraphrase of Psalm 23, with the added words and phrases italicized:

The God *of love* my Shepherd is,
And he that doth me feed;
*While He is mine and I am His,*
What can I want *or need*?

He leads me to the *tender* grass,
Where I *both feed and* rest;
Then to the streams that gently pass,
*In both I have the best.* . . .

Yea, in death's shady, black *abode*
Well may I walk, not fear,
For Thou art with me, and Thy rod
*To guide,* Thy staff *to bear.*

What do hymn writers do when they paraphrase a psalm? They expand and clarify beyond what the original text says, and occasionally they substitute words for what is in the original text ("abode" instead of "valley").

Chart 9.1 (on page 106) is a sampling of how dynamic equivalent translations render specimens (right column, and with added or substituted elements italicized), as compared with an essentially literal rendition of the same passage (left column).

It is obvious that in these specimens dynamic equivalent translators do exactly what hymn writers do: they paraphrase by adding explanatory material beyond what the original does, and they substitute terms for what the original contains. Someone has correctly compared the effect of dynamic equivalent translations to that of "hearing a poet read his verses while someone stands by and paraphrases."[4] As for having confidence that we know what the original actually says, the situation is hopeless.

The passages quoted in the left column confirm what we know to be true of essentially literal translations: they do not add, subtract, and substitute as dynamic equivalent translations regularly do. Instead they stick to verbal correspondence—finding

**Chart 9.1 How Dynamic Equivalent Translations Are Actually Paraphrases**

| Psalm 34:5a | |
|---|---|
| "Those who look to him are radiant." | *"The oppressed* look to him and are *glad."* (GNB) |
| | "Those who look to him *for help* will be radiant *with joy."* (NLT) |
| | *"Keep your eyes on the* Lᴏʀᴅ! / You will shine *like the sun."* (CEV) |
| **Psalm 23:5b** | |
| "My cup overflows." | "My cup overflows *with blessings."* (NLT) |
| | *"You . . . fill* my cup *until it* overflows." (CEV) |
| **Mark 9:50a** | |
| "Have salt in yourselves." | "Have the salt *of friendship among* yourselves." (GNB) |
| | "Have salt *among* you." (CEV) |
| | "You *must* have *the qualities of* salt *among* yourselves." (NLT) |
| | *"Be preservatives* yourselves." (MESSAGE) |

the English words and phrases that correspond to the words of the original.

---

"This is certainly not a translation. It is almost a homily; useful in its place, but misleading to one who seeks the words of the Author." —Francis R. Steele, on the technique of paraphrase

---

**Chapter Summary**

This chapter has been an initial foray into the differences between essentially literal and dynamic equivalent translations. Ideas do have consequences. In the illustrations that I adduced, it is easy to see the difference between faithfulness to the words of the original and a translation that feels free to move beyond those words. The difference between translators who paraphrase and those who do not is equally apparent.

# 10

# DIVERGENT STYLES

# OF TRANSLATION

THIS IS THE SECOND CHAPTER in which I provide illustrations of how the two theories of translation actually influence the translation process. *Style* is an admittedly amorphous term, but we know that it is a combination of vocabulary, syntax (sentence structure), and patterning of phrases and clauses. While definitions of style are elusive, we all experience the qualities of style the moment we read or hear a piece of writing.

## Formal versus Colloquial Styles

Eugene Nida is fond of the anecdote about the reader of Today's English Version who exclaimed, "This must not be the Bible; I can understand it."[1] A translation should of course be understandable to an English reader, but it is a fair inference that the reader who was quoted was commenting on the colloquial style in which the translation is couched. In my sojourns through the writing of dynamic equivalent proponents, I repeatedly ran across the sentiment that a modern translation should not "sound like the Bible." Gordon Fee and Mark Strauss, for example, stigmatize translations that use "traditional Bible language" with the labels "Biblish or 'Bible-ese.'"[2]

Although essentially literal advocates do not ordinarily express the viewpoint that an English translation should "sound like the Bible," they nonetheless believe the Bible should not sound like a teenager's account of last evening's ballgame. It should instead possess what translations in the King James tradition possess—formality, dignity, an appropriate strand of archaism, and exaltation. In later chapters I will explain why I believe an English Bible should possess these qualities. In this chapter my purpose is mainly to illustrate the contrasting styles of English Bibles.

### Translating Poetry

Here is an essentially literal version of Psalm 103:1–5:

> Bless the LORD, O my soul,
>     and all that is within me,
>     bless his holy name!
> Bless the LORD, O my soul,
>     and forget not all his benefits,
> who forgives all your iniquity,
>     who heals all your diseases,
> who redeems your life from the pit,
>     who crowns you with steadfast love and mercy,
> who satisfies you with good
>     so that your youth is renewed like the eagle's.

This poetic passage is expressed in the high style and does not sound like ordinary conversation. It is couched in the verse form of parallelism, with the second and third lines repeating the general idea of the opening line, but with added exaltation. The centerpiece of artistry in the passage is the five successive parallel "who" clauses, an obviously embellished, ornate rhetorical pattern.

The NIV represents a halfway step toward informality. It substitutes the more contemporary *praise* for *bless* in the opening command to the speaker's soul. The all-encompassing "all that is within me" becomes toned down to a more modern-sounding "all my inmost being." The biggest change, though, is that instead of preserving the five parallel "who" clauses, the translators introduced a coordinate *and* to produce pairs of clauses (for example, "who forgives all your sins *and* heals all your diseases"). That is enough to push a highly poetic and rhetorically stylized passage in the direction of a prose statement.

This drift toward colloquial prose becomes complete with such dynamic equivalent renditions as we find in the Contemporary English Version and *The Message*. In these two, the formal-sounding "forget not all his benefits" becomes "I will never forget how kind he has been" and "don't forget a single blessing!" The clause "who satisfies you with good" is rendered "each day that we live, he provides for our needs" (CEV) and "he wraps you in goodness—beauty eternal" (MESSAGE).

### Translating Prose Narrative

Narrative style provides an equally good point of comparison. Here is a dramatic exchange between Adonijah and Bathsheba in an essentially literal translation: "Then Adonijah the son of Haggith came to Bathsheba the mother of Solomon. And she said, 'Do you come peacefully?' He said, 'Peacefully.' Then he said, 'I have something to say to you.' She said, 'Speak'" (1 Kings 2:13–14, ESV). Before I quote the same passage from a colloquial translation, I want to insist that court figures in ancient societies spoke according to high standards of etiquette and protocol. Even commoners who rose to the top were characterized by good speech—witness the commendation of David to Saul that "he speaks well" (1 Sam. 16:18, NIV). Furthermore, modern standards of colloquial discourse in which speakers can scarcely finish a sentence without adding the fillers "like" and "you know" came on the scene only relatively recently.

Here is the exchange between courtier and queen in a colloquial translation: "One day, Adonijah went to see Bathsheba, Solomon's mother, and she asked, 'Is this a friendly visit?' 'Yes. I just want to talk with you.' 'All right,' she told him, 'go ahead.'"

(1 Kings 2:13–14, CEV). This is the idiom of the grocery store, and it illustrates the stylistic preference of a modern colloquial translation.

---

Here are specimens of how people who dislike colloquial translations have expressed their response:
- "The exalted has become flat, the pungent bland, the rhythm crippled." —Dwight Macdonald, in an essay entitled "The Bible in Modern Undress"
- "Too often it is as if [modern translators] were officiating in Westminster Abbey in shirtsleeves. . . . That kind of familiarity, too, can breed contempt."—F. L. Lucas
- ". . . a symptom of the decay of the English language" and "an active agent of decadence."—T. S. Eliot, commenting on the language of the New English Bible

---

## The Quest for a Colloquial Bible

The issue is not simply that dynamic equivalent translators want a Bible that sounds like everyday *contemporary* discourse, because contemporary discourse can be formal as well as informal. What dynamic equivalent translations deliver in addition is a *colloquial* or informal style based on *oral* speech patterns rather than *written* discourse. Specimens like the following are what we might hear across the backyard fence, *not* what we read in *Newsweek* or the daily newspaper: "Eliab . . . became angry with David and said, 'What are you doing here? . . . You smart aleck, you! You just came to watch the fighting!'" (1 Sam. 17:28, GNB). "Does some stupid person want proof that faith without deeds is useless?" (James 2:20, CEV). "It's terribly unfair for the same thing to happen to each of us" (Eccl. 9:3, CEV). "If one of you wants to be number one, he should be in last place" (Mark 9:35, SEB). "Dear friend, if you've gone into hock with your neighbor / or locked yourself in a deal with a stranger, / . . . don't waste a minute, get yourself out of that mess" (Prov. 6:1, 3, MESSAGE).

110

It is obvious that modern translations exist on a stylistic continuum. On one end we have a Bible that does, in significant ways, "sound like the Bible." On the other end we have the oral speech of conversation at the bus stop.

## Concrete versus Abstract Vocabulary

Another major divide separating the styles of the two kinds of translation is the contrast between concrete and abstract vocabulary. The vocabulary of the original biblical text is strikingly concrete, especially in the Hebrew Old Testament. Literary discourse, moreover, prefers the concrete to the abstract, and the Bible is a literary anthology. The cliché in creative writing classes is that the writer "must show rather than tell," that is, embody meaning in concrete rather than abstract form.

### A Fondness for Abstraction in Dynamic Equivalent Translations

Essentially literal translations tend to preserve the concreteness of the original text, while dynamic equivalent translations are continually pulling the text in the direction of abstraction. The story of Cain opens with what in modern literary terminology we would call a sex scene and birth scene: "Now Adam knew Eve his wife, and she conceived and bore Cain" (Gen. 4:1, ESV). This gives us a sense of the stuff of real life. But the concrete has become abstract when we read that "Adam and Eve had a son" (CEV). In the same vein, we can contrast the vividness and specificity of "Samuel hacked Agag to pieces before the LORD" (1 Sam. 15:33, ESV) to the abstractness of "Samuel put Agag to death before the LORD" (NIV).

Paul's metaphor of life as a *walk* down a path provides a litmus test of the two styles of translating. Essentially literal translations render 1 Thessalonians 2:12 "walk in a manner worthy of God" (NASB, ESV; KJV, NKJV also retain the verb *walk*). Dynamic equivalent translations opt for the more generalized and non-metaphoric *live* (NIV, NLT, GNB, REB, CEV, TNIV).

111

Literary authors and teachers of writing are virtually unanimous in their agreement that good writing ordinarily is concrete and specific rather than abstract and generalized. Here are specimen statements:

- Good writing is "the trick—and to some minds the scandal—of particularity."—Dorothy Sayers
- "The beginning of human knowledge is through the senses, and the fiction writer begins where human perception begins. He appeals through the senses. . . . The first and most obvious characteristic of fiction is that it deals with reality through what can be seen, heard, smelt, tasted, and touched."—Flannery O'Connor
- "From Homer, who never omits to tell us that the ships were black and the sea salt, or even wet, . . . Poets are always telling us that grass is green, or thunder loud, or lips red."—C. S. Lewis
- "The poet uses images and sensations much more than he uses abstract ideas."—Northrop Frye
- "The writers of the Old Testament—and to a lesser degree those of the New as well—thought and felt and spoke in images—in a vocabulary compact of nearly all the physical sensations that flesh is heir to."—Jonathan Livingston Lowes

In literal versions, Paul speaks of "a wide door" opening for him (1 Cor. 16:9); in some dynamic equivalent versions the door becomes "a good opportunity" (NCV) or "a wonderful opportunity" (CEV) or "a real opportunity" (GNB). The evocative "land flowing with milk and honey" (e.g., Ex. 3:8) becomes "a fertile land" (NCV) or "rich and fertile" (GNB). The concrete "finger of God" (Luke 11:20) becomes the abstract "power" of God (CEV, GNB, NCV). Jesus said, "Blessed are those who hunger and thirst for righteousness" (Matt. 5:6, ESV); "happy are those whose greatest desire is to do what God requires," the GNB says abstractly.

Of course the poetic parts of the Bible provide the greatest scope for retaining or removing the concrete imagery of the original text. "You know when I sit down and when I rise up," says an essentially literal rendition of Psalm 139:2. The images here are visual. Dynamic equivalent translations prefer abstraction. In the Good News Bible, the sitting and rising become the generalized "everything I do." Another translation substitutes "resting" for sitting and "working" for rising up (CEV). Both of the latter two are moves in the direction of abstraction. The next verse reads, "You search out my path and my lying down" (Ps. 139:3, ESV). The CEV generalizes those visual images as "you notice everything I do," the REB as "journeying and . . . resting-places," and *The Message* as "leave" and "get back."

## The Reason for the Preference of the Abstract

I am not saying that dynamic equivalent translations remove *most* of the concreteness of the Bible. In the narrative parts of the Bible, dynamic equivalent translations are often very vivid— sometimes more vivid than the original. But dynamic equivalent translators *do not hesitate* to turn concrete language, including poetic imagery, into abstractions.

It is easy to see why they do this. One reason is that most dynamic equivalent translators do not assign a high priority to the literary qualities of the Bible (as I will show in a later chapter). Literature is inherently concrete. If one does not grant primacy to retaining the literary quality of the Bible, it is no great matter to forego the concrete language of the original.

That, in turn, is intensified by the preoccupation of dynamic equivalent translators to *explain* and *interpret* the statements of the Bible so that a reader does not need to do the interpreting. Given that orientation, it is inevitable that a prevailing impulse toward abstraction hovers over dynamic equivalent translations.

## Preserving versus Changing the Style of the Original Text

Running parallel to the contrasting styles in English translation are the attitudes that translators hold regarding the style of the Bible in its original language. Of particular importance are the idiomatic expressions in the original text—ways of expressing something that seem natural to native speakers of a language but that are actually figurative or formulaic and therefore perplexing or strange to a nonnative speaker. The longer I deal with the translation debate, the more central this issue seems to me.

## Sexual Euphemisms as a Test Case

Before I analyze the matter, it will help simply to put an example on the table. A Hebrew euphemism for sexual union between husband and wife is the verb *knew*—for example, "Adam knew Eve his wife, and she conceived" (Gen. 4:1, as rendered in all essentially literal translations). English translators immediately divide in their attitudes toward such idiomatic expressions.

Dynamic equivalent translators assume that such expressions are quirks of the original language—strange ways of expressing something that are "accidents" of that language. These translators accordingly cannot abide the thought of retaining them when they translate. Thus the euphemism *knew* is translated as "lay with" (multiple translations), "had intercourse with" (GNB), or—in the most ridiculous of all modern euphemisms—"slept with" (NLT). Behind all of these translations lies the assumption that the idiomatic expression *knew* cannot possibly be valid for us today; it is an aberration of the original language, and the fact that "we would not say it that way" (the ever-present motto of dynamic equivalent translators) means that "it needs to go."

My own bent is exactly the opposite of that. I begin with an awareness that most words in all languages were originally metaphoric. Words that are now abstractions were originally concrete, as a perusal of the etymology of words in a dictionary will show. As a person who respects literature, I take metaphoric language very seriously.

Instead of assuming that a strange way of saying something is automatically inferior—a linguistic mistake that needs to be corrected—I begin with the opposite premise that "there is something here for me." I am immediately open to the possibility that the strange formulation might actually contain rich meanings and insights that will unfold if only I take time to ponder a statement. When I ponder, I find that the euphemism *knew* for sexual intimacy between husband and wife contains a wealth of insight, whereas the replacement formulations "lay with," "had sexual intercourse with," "had sex," and "slept with" emphatically do not.

Owen Barfield is a classic source on the originally concrete and metaphoric nature of most words in the English language: "If we trace the meanings of a great many words . . . as far back as etymology can take us, we are at once made to realize that an overwhelming proportion, if not all, of them referred in earlier days to one of these two things—a solid, sensible object, or some animal (probably human) activity. Examples abound on every page of the dictionary."

## The Practical Implications for Translation

There is no way to reconcile these two viewpoints and the resulting styles of translation. Dynamic equivalent translators can hardly wait to get the offensive idiomatic expressions off the board. In the Old Testament historical books, it is a common idiom to say that a given king "slept with his fathers" (e.g., 1 Kings 2:10). The preface to the New Living Translation singles out this idiom for attention, claiming that in translating the idiom as "died," the translation is the "only" one that "clearly translates the real meaning of the Hebrew idiom . . . into contemporary English."

Essentially literal translators disagree. Instead of beginning with the premise that the ancient formulation is faulty and our familiar modern one superior, they reverse that assumption. Pondering the ancient formula "slept with his fathers" yields such ideas as continuity of generations, acknowledgment that death is the common human fate, perhaps a reference to the patriarchal past in the word *fathers*, and the mystery of death as captured in calling it a metaphoric "sleep."

We read in Matthew 1:23 that "they shall call his name Immanuel." A dynamic equivalent proponent writes that "when a child is born into the home of an English speaker, we may 'call' the child John or Bill, or 'name' him John or Bill; but we *never* 'call his name' John or Bill."[3] And *because* we do not, claims this writer, it cannot possibly be correct to retain the ancient way of saying it. An essentially literal translator will retain the formulation, in the expectation that readers will ponder the statement because of its very strangeness. And when they ponder, they begin to see that the importance that ancient cultures attached to a *name* is here combined with a reminder that names are consciously chosen and conferred by people who *called* a person by that name.

This is not to deny that many, many constructions in Hebrew and Greek just naturally get modified when they are translated into clear English. If Matthew 1:18 says that Mary was in a state of "having in belly," then of course that gets translated as "with child" or "pregnant." But essentially literal translators do not agree with the easy *dismissal* that their counterparts make when confronted with an idiomatic expression.

Because we do not say "he opened his mouth and taught them" (Matt. 5:2), dynamic equivalent translators conclude that to translate it "he began to teach them" renders the Greek "accurately," while translations that retain the original construction "introduce an unnatural English expression."[4] But wait a minute: "opened his mouth" not only makes the scene come alive in our imaginations with a visual picture—it also identifies the situation as an oral speech act, something that "began" does not. Furthermore, the old formula signaled something to the effect, "What I am about to say is *really important*," a meaning that gets lost in the flat "began." Finally, we still use expressions similar to the one found in Matthew 5:2: "I want you to keep your mouth shut" and "he should never have opened his mouth."

## Implications for How We View the Bible

In an earlier chapter I spoke of the diminished respect for the Bible and its authors that I believe has accompanied the theory and practice of dynamic equivalent translation. If we are continuously told that the Bible in its original form is an eccentric text that more or less continually needs to be corrected in its queer ways of expressing its content, it is natural to start thinking of the Bible as a strange and deficient book.

For dynamic equivalent translators, the crucial question is "how we would say it." For essentially literal translators, the important question is how the original authors *did* say it. We are right back to a question that I posed in an earlier chapter,

116

namely, should translators deliver the Bible as an ancient book or a modern book?

The fact that an essentially literal translation presents the reader with something unfamiliar helps preserve the Bible's ability to stand over against familiar assumptions, whereas a translation that slides easily into the modern mind also slides out easily. More important, though, is the frequency with which a modern-sounding translation gives us something that isn't even in the original text—or *omits* something that *is* in the original text.

## Chapter Summary

The contrasting styles of the two kinds of translation are apparent the moment we start reading an English Bible. We quickly see stylistic preferences at work—preferences of either colloquial or formal styles, and of abstract or concrete language. And in regard to removing strange-sounding ancient ways of saying something versus retaining as much of the original wording as clarity allows, the two translation styles are simply on a collision course.

PART FOUR

# The Ideal English Bible Translation

Up to this point I have explored the differences between the two translation philosophies and practices that currently divide the world of Bible translation between them. Although it has been obvious that I favor essentially literal translation over dynamic equivalence, I have not systematically considered the question of what constitutes the ideal English Bible. I am ready to turn to that task.

I have, of course, already said something about one of the qualities that make up the right Bible translation, namely, the preservation of the words of the original to the extent that English language and syntax allow. I can think of no other reason to read an English translation than to be taken as close as possible to what the original authors of the Bible actually said. I do not want a translation committee's filtered version of the original text; I want the original text. I want the real or actual Bible, not a substitute Bible.

# 11

# FULLNESS RATHER THAN
# REDUCTIONISM

THE PREFACE to the New King James Version uses an excellent formula when it speaks of "full equivalence." Here is the statement: "This principle of complete equivalence seeks to preserve *all* of the information in the text, while presenting it in good literary form." The very next sentence in the preface contrasts this ideal to dynamic equivalence as a form of translation. This chapter represents my fleshing out of what the NKJV preface announces.

The ideal of fullness that I sketch in this chapter is something that translations in the Tyndale–King James tradition have always assumed and perpetuated. It was not until dynamic equivalent translations introduced certain forms of reductionism that essentially literal proponents found it necessary to define their theory and practice of full equivalence.

I have already discussed several types of reductionism that lie at the heart of the dynamic equivalence experiment. They include a reduced estimate of Bible readers' linguistic and intellectual abilities, and a reduced respect for the adequacy of biblical authors and texts to express their content in a form that modern readers can understand. I will not retread that territory in this chapter. In a later chapter I will discuss the reduced literary qualities of dynamic equivalent translations. In this chapter I will cover three additional types of reductionism: reduced vocabulary, reduction of exegetical scope for the biblical text, and decreased theological substance. Those kinds of reductionism are the background against which I will advocate the ideal of fullness.

## "High Thoughts Must Have High Language"

The Greek playwright Aristophanes said something profound when he stated the principle that "high thoughts must have high language."[1] Colloquial and contemporizing translations do not believe it; translations in the King James tradition embody it.

In an earlier chapter I noted the preference of dynamic equivalent translators to produce a style that approximates everyday oral speech patterns. My point there was mainly to describe rather than assess this phenomenon and to view it as a stylistic preference rather than something that affects the content of an utterance. But style is substance, and in this section I propose to analyze what happens to biblical content when vocabulary is scaled downward.

### From Woman of Worth to Fine Woman

In the midnight encounter of Ruth and Boaz on the threshing floor, Boaz commends the worthiness of Ruth with the statement, "all my fellow townsmen know that you are a woman of worth" (Ruth 3:11, RSV). "A woman of worth"—this is a stately epithet, a title for a person or thing. The effect is to elevate Ruth above the commonplace to the heroic status that the story as a whole accords to her. Two other modern renditions maintain this same grandeur: "a worthy woman" (ESV, NRSV) and "a woman of noble character" (NIV).

As we move down the scale of increasing colloquialism in the following renditions, the stature of Ruth progressively shrinks: "you are respected by everyone in town" (CEV); "as everyone in town knows, you are a fine woman" (GNB); "the whole town knows what a fine woman you are" (REB); "as the whole neighbourhood knows, you are a capable woman" (NEB); "everyone knows what a wonderful person you are" (TLB); "everybody in town knows what a courageous woman you are—a real prize" (MESSAGE). High thoughts require high words; if we shrink the words, the substance also diminishes.

---

Tyndale and the King James Bible were the major influences in establishing the English language in its former glory, while modern translations have contributed to the impoverishment of the language:

- "Tyndale's gift to the English language was unmeasurable. . . . There is truth in the remark 'without Tyndale, no Shakespeare.'"—David Daniell
- "One of the unintended functions of the King James Bible was to establish norms in written and spoken English. . . . The King James Bible was . . . to exercise a substantial and decisive influence over the shaping of the English language."—Alister McGrath
- "We ask in alarm, 'What is happening to the English language [in modern Bible translations]?' . . . It is as much our business to attempt to arrest deterioration and combat corruption of our language, as to accept change." Modern Bible translations are "an active agent of decadence" in language.—T. S. Eliot
- "I believe the Christian Church has a profound responsibility towards a people's language. . . . It is as serious a matter to corrupt a people's language as it is to corrupt a people's behaviour."—Martin Jarrett-Kerr

---

### From Men of Valor to a Group of Men

The Old Testament historical chronicles about kings and queens were written by court historians. If their writings fall just a little short of ranking as epics, they are nonetheless not far from that. Accordingly, the writers pitch their writing at a relatively high level. My heart always thrills when I read about the good advisors with whom King Saul initially surrounded himself: "men of valor whose hearts God had touched" (1 Sam. 10:26, RSV, ESV). "Men of valor" is an epithet whose grandeur is commensurate with the men they name. "Valiant men" also makes the grade (NKJV, NIV, NASB).

But as the vocabulary is reduced, the men who supported Saul as an initially worthy king become progressively ordinary. A first wave of diminishment occurs with such translations as "powerful men" (GNB), "warriors" (NRSV), and "true and brave men" (MESSAGE). Finally we end with "strong men" (NLV), "young men" (CEV), "fighting men" (REB), and "band of men" (NLT). In the CEV version, moreover, the men do not have hearts touched by God but are simply young men whom "God had encouraged . . . to become followers of Saul."

### From Prophetic Oracle to a Bit of Advice

The Old Testament prophets were not plainspoken people. They were masters of oratory. They usually spoke in poetic form rather than straightforward prose. Rhetorical patterning is common in their discourses, and they often used such devices as rhetorical questions, epithets (titles for persons or things), and authoritative commands from God. The most customary genre in which these heightened discourses are embodied is the oracle—an authoritative pronouncement from God.

One of the greatest oracles from Old Testament prophecy is Samuel's rebuke to King Saul in 1 Samuel 15:22:

> Has the LORD as great delight in burnt offerings and
> sacrifices,
>    as in obeying the voice of the LORD?
> Behold, to obey is better than sacrifice,
>    and to listen than the fat of rams. (ESV)

I am so glad that I had the King James Bible from which to memorize that verse as an eight-year-old. I did not know what all the words meant, but I knew that the statement was an awe-inspiring principle on which one could build a life. I also intuitively sensed that someday I would understand the full meaning of the statement. Today, a youngster might be presented with something like this:

"Tell me," Samuel said. "Does the LORD really want sacrifices and offerings? No! He doesn't want your sacrifices. He wants you to obey him." (CEV)

That rendition is considerably less than oracular. Nor is it how a prophet would address a king in an ancient monarchical context. In *The Message*, we hear Samuel say that God "wants you to listen to him! Plain listening is the thing, not staging a lavish religious production."

### Summary: Linguistic Reduction

I do not want to exaggerate the extent to which contemporizing translations scale back the language of the Bible. As in touring a bombed out cathedral, it is often surprising to see what remains of the original edifice. But neither should we minimize the linguistic reduction that has occurred with the dynamic equivalent movement.

The commitment to phrase things in an informal style pitched at a modest linguistic level is expressed in the prefaces and theoretic statements of the movement, and simply dipping into any modernizing translation shows the principle at work. By contrast—and this is the first cornerstone in my description of an ideal English translation—a good translation gives us words and sentences that have substance.

### Preserving the Full Exegetical Potential of the Bible

A second type of fullness that a good translation possesses goes by the formidable name of preserving the full exegetical potential of the biblical text. One dimension of this is that the translators have not made preemptive interpretive strikes that remove potential meanings from the Bible. Another aspect is that where a passage possesses legitimate multiple meanings, the translators phrase matters in such a way as to allow all of those meanings to be drawn from the text.

Poetry is a continuous test of where a translation falls on this issue. Essentially literal translations preserve the poetic form with all of its interpretive options and difficulties; dynamic equivalent translations often (though not always) narrow the interpretive options to one, either by removing metaphors from sight or adding interpretive commentary that names just one possibility.

"All my springs are in you," the poet says in Psalm 87:7 (ESV and other literal translations; NIV, "fountains"). Metaphors are always an invitation to discover the meanings of a statement, and nearly all metaphors have multiple "carry-overs" (the literal meaning of the word *metaphor*) to the actual subject of the utterance. The first quality of a spring is that it is a source of water and additionally *a continuous or permanent* source of it. Water, in turn, embodies multiple meanings, including refreshment and the sustaining of life. A spring or fountain of water, in turn, entails an aesthetic sense of beauty and also evokes an emotional sense of well-being and peacefulness.

To preserve the full exegetical potential of Psalm 87:7 requires a translator to put the metaphor of spring or fountain in front of a reader in its untouched form. But the general bent of dynamic equivalent translators is to be afraid of anything that will tax a reader. One way to eliminate strain for a reader is to remove the metaphor and replace it with direct statement: "source of all our blessings" (GNB); "I too am from Zion" (CEV); "all good things come from Jerusalem" (NCV). The alternate way of narrowing down the statement to a single meaning is to pair the metaphoric spring or fountain with an abstraction: "springs *of joy*" (NASB); "the *source of my life* springs from Jerusalem" (NLT). The opposite of preserving the full exegetical potential of the Bible is to narrow it down to a one-dimensional Bible, and dynamic equivalence often does just that.

---

- "A translation of the Bible . . . should aim to retain, as far as possible, the exegetical potential of the [source text]."—Anthony A. Nichols
- Translators who remove legitimate interpretive options "may have replaced God's word with their own."—Raymond C. Van Leeuwen

Poetry, though, is not the only genre in the Bible where dynamic equivalent translators perform their preemptive strikes and interpretive overlay. Second Corinthians 5:14 states, "The love of Christ controls us" (RSV, NASB, NKJV, REB, ESV). Does this mean "our love for Christ" or "Christ's love for us?" Probably both, but in any case the original leaves the door open to both interpretations. Essentially literal translations preserve the full exegetical potential of the text. But dynamic equivalent translations are unwilling to pass the full range of possible meanings to readers. They accordingly render it "Christ's love" (NIV, CEV, NLT).

In 1 John 2:5 we read regarding believers who keep God's Word that "the love of God" is perfected in them (NKJV, NASB, ESV). In the original, that phrase can refer either to God's love for the believer or the believer's love for God, or both. Preserving the full exegetical potential of the text requires leaving the options open to the interpreter. One-dimensional translations are unwilling to do that. They translate it either "God's love" (NIV) or "love for God" (RSV, GNB; NLT and CEV also phrase the verse in such a way as to allow only that interpretation).

### Summary: Preserving Full Exegetical Potential

The translation philosophy of full equivalence is committed to giving Bible readers the full range of interpretive options that the original possesses. Dynamic equivalent translators begin with two premises in this regard: (a) translators know best, and (b) readers cannot deal adequately with ambiguity or multiple meanings.[2] Based on those premises, dynamic equivalent translations make up readers' minds for them, and readers, of course, have no way of knowing that this preemptive interpretive strike has been made. Raymond Van Leeuwen correctly labels such translations as "'closed' rather than 'open' because they shut down the process of wrestling with what God has said. . . . By choosing one meaning and rejecting another, they close the door to reflection and new insight."[3]

## Theological Fullness

Not all dynamic equivalent translations are equally guilty of removing theological language from the Bible, so the stricture that I am about to explore applies to some but not all dynamic equivalent translations. Some dynamic equivalent prefaces clarify that theological vocabulary has been removed, while others simply remove it. An examination of the text itself shows that the CEV avoided "traditionally theological language . . . like 'atonement,' 'redemption,' 'righteousness' and 'sanctification.'"[4] A member of the American Bible Society claimed that the Good News Bible was designed for the "unsophisticated" or "average" reader, who would be grateful for "being delivered from theological subtleties."[5] The Simple English Bible confirms in its preface that the translators excised "religious words" like *"baptism, church, justification, redemption, etc."*

A good translation retains theological vocabulary commensurate with the original. To see why this is a criterion of good translation, we need to consider what happens when theological words are dropped. Galatians 2:16 states, "We know that a person is not justified by works of the law but through faith in Jesus Christ." Translations that are committed to the avoidance of the theological term *justified* or *justification* offer as substitutes "made right with God" (NLT), "set right before God" (MESSAGE), "God accepts those" (CEV), and "put right with God" (GNB).

---

- "The simple translation makes the Bible easy to understand at the expense of there being a lot less to understand."—Noel K. Weeks
- "Ditching 'traditional theological language' can easily slide into ditching theology."—David Daniell

---

There are at least two reasons why a translation should retain traditional theological language. The first is that while there may be no *a priori* reason for alternatives to fall short of the theological fullness of traditional terms, the substitutes are almost always reductionistic. First John 2:2 states that Christ is "the propitiation for our sins" (NASB, NKJV, ESV). The word *propitiation* means

128

"to appease anger through the offering of a sacrifice." None of the dynamic equivalent substitutions for the word *propitiation* encompasses the fullness of that word: "died in our place" (NCV), "paid for our sins" (NLV), "the sacrifice" (CEV), "the sacrifice that atones" (NLT), "atoning sacrifice" (NIV), "the means by which our sins are forgiven" (GNB). When we shrink our theological vocabulary, we shrink our theological understanding.

Second, it is simply the case that theological discourse derives from the terms that we find in the Bible. I have yet to see a theology book that speaks of "the doctrine of being put right with God." The theological language of the Bible needs to match the language of our theology books. When theological terms drop out of our Bibles, the theological categories also disappear.

As with so many of the dynamic equivalent moves that I deplore, dropping the word *justifies* is so unnecessary. The word is part of our active vocabulary: "I wonder how she will justify that decision"; "the end does not justify the means." A word processor requires us to choose between "ragged" and "justified" margins. Again and again dynamic equivalent translators ask us to operate at a lower level with the Bible than we do in the rest of life.

## Summary: Theological Fullness

The ideal English Bible retains as much of the original text as the process of translation allows, including fullness of language, fullness of interpretive meanings, and fullness of theological vocabulary. Such a Bible results only when translators reject claims that translators possess such superior knowledge that they are free to remove details from the original text or add details during the process of translation.

# 12

# TRANSPARENCY

# TO THE ORIGINAL TEXT

WHEN DYNAMIC equivalent translators speak of transparency, they mean transparency to a modern reader. To achieve it, translators make all changes to the original text required to produce an English translation easily understandable to an English-speaking reader with modest reading and comprehension abilities. When a translation committee with this viewpoint does its daily work, decisions are made with a perceived modern reader in view.

By contrast, committees that accept an essentially literal translation philosophy keep their eye on what the original text says. Once they have determined that, they choose the vocabulary that most closely corresponds to the original text. Their goal is to provide the clearest "window" through which a reader can see what the original authors wrote and (equally importantly) what the original readers would have understood as they read or heard the original text.

These two conceptions of transparency cannot be consistently reconciled during the process of translation. At many points they are on a collision course. I accept the premise that the purpose of an English Bible translation is to allow a reader to look directly at what the authors of the Bible said and thought. In pursuing my argument, I will (1) explain the concept of transparency to the original text, (2) illustrate the difference between translations that provide such transparency and those that do not, and (3) provide reasons to believe that the ideal English translation provides the kind of transparency that I have described and illustrated.

## Defining the Ideal of Transparency

Whenever we sit down to read something, we enter a "world" of the mind or imagination. This is true of any piece of writing, even if it is contemporary—in fact, even if it is a story set in our hometown. But we are often more aware of the world of the text when the text comes to us from a time and place far removed from us. In such an instance, we are continuously aware of the strangeness of the world that we have entered.

Literary scholars stress the world of the text as the key to its meaning. Flannery O'Conner has the best statement: "It is from the kind of world the writer creates, from the kind of character and detail he invests it with, that a reader can find *the intellectual meaning* of a book."[1] Biblical scholars operate with the same premise: "The Bible creates a world of meaning, and we need to enter it and make ourselves at home in its strangeness, all the better to understand our world, which is insufficiently strange to us. In this indirect way, the Bible, and our Lord who speaks in and through it, still speak to us today."[2]

Biblical interpretation is a two-way journey. First we travel *to* the world of the biblical text. Then we make a return trip *from* the world of the biblical text to our own time and place. The way to our hometown is through Jerusalem.

But it is this very principle that has produced some of the greatest divergence among the rival translation philosophies. Essentially literal translators believe that it is the proper role of a Bible translation to facilitate the journey to the world of the biblical text and to allow a reader to live within that world.

Dynamic equivalent translations often (not always) update references in such a way as to short-circuit the journey to the world of the biblical text.

## Ways of Preserving the World of the Original Text

Even though my goal in this section of the book is to delineate the ideal English Bible, it is impossible to do only that. Given the context of modern Bible translation, the case for essentially literal translation always needs to be argued in an awareness of the contrary claims that dynamic equivalent translators continually hold before the Bible-reading public.

### White Garments and Oil or Fine Clothes and Cologne?

In Ecclesiastes 9:8, the poet uses ancient imagery of joy and festivity when he commands, "Let your garments be always white. Let not oil be lacking on your head" (ESV; other literal translations similar). Modern readers doubtless need an initial explanatory note from a preacher or commentator to inform them that white garments and oil on the head were external signs of celebration and joy in ancient cultures. And when readers learn that, they experience a pleasant addition to their fund of knowledge and a salutary reminder that not everyone who has lived has done things the way we do them. Furthermore, once readers are alerted to the meaning of the white garments and oil on the head, they will keep encountering these images in the pages of the Bible, whereas if these images are removed from Ecclesiastes 9:8, readers will be deprived of the cross references that build up during the course of reading the Bible.

By contrast, here is how a dynamic equivalent translation renders the verse: "Wear fine clothes, with a splash of cologne" (NLT). The abstraction "fine clothes" is universal and makes no appeal to the imagination (our image-making capacity). The generic "fine clothes" does not transport us to an ancient world where white garments signaled celebration. The image of cologne keeps us rooted right in the modern Western world and in that very process prevents us from traveling to the world of the original text.

- "There is today a general religious bias toward a galloping subjectivity. But our first obligation to a text is to let it hang there in celestial objectivity—not to ask what it means to us. . . . The text had a particular meaning before I saw it, and it will continue to mean that after I have seen it. It expresses an intention . . . [free from] any one individual's preferences or biases."—Joseph Sittler
- "The serious reader of a translation cannot forego the obligation of learning the text's 'world' of natural and cultural realities, its characters and world-view."—Raymond C. Van Leeuwen

## A Table Full of Fatness versus a Table of Your Favorite Food

One dimension of the world of the biblical text is the mind-set and worldview of the original author and audience. While there is much that is universal in the Bible, there is also much that differs from our own outlook. For example, the ancient world, with its subsistence economy, had a view of fat that is the opposite of that of most Westerners. Whereas to us fatness is feared as something unhealthy, for people living in a subsistence economy fatness is a status symbol, signaling that a person is prosperous enough to eat in such a way as to become fat. (Incidentally, the Lewis and Clark chronicles reveal that the explorers got very tired of lean meat and were overjoyed when they finally got their teeth into some fat-laden beaver tails and buffalo tongues.)

Literature from the ancient world freely uses fat as the literal image for abundance. The picture of God-sent human prosperity that Elihu paints in Job 36 includes the detail that "what was set on your table was full of fatness" (v. 16, RSV, NRSV, ESV; similar in KJV). As readers of an ancient text, we need the world of the text retained in such a detail. Quite apart from meeting the literary criterion of concrete and vivid expression, it alerts us to the kind of world that the ancient world was, with its relative impoverishment by modern Western standards.

Being kept conscious of the subsistence economy of the biblical world makes a lot fall into place, including the ethical commands of the Bible (such as the command not to keep a poor person's coat overnight because it was the only coat he or she owned). But some translations conceal the actual world of the biblical text from their readers. Instead of reading about a table full of fatness, we get such vague renditions as "you have prospered" (NLT), "a generous table" (REB), "your table laden with choice food" (NIV), "your table with your favorite food" (CEV), "rich food piled high on your table" (JB). Some of these translations encourage a modern reader to fill in the picture of what a choice meal looks like in a modern setting, and imperceptibly the biblical world has become the modern affluent West. The problem with excising the ancient aura from the Bible and translating as much as possible into a contemporary counterpart is that translators—and readers after them—impose their own worldview on the Bible instead of allowing the Bible to shape the reader's worldview.

### Stylistics as Part of the World of the Original Text

The examples that I have cited thus far fall into the categories of the customs that made up the biblical world and the mind set or worldview of people living in the world of the Bible. An additional dimension is the style in which the writers of the Bible expressed their content. In a general way these stylistic traits can keep alive our awareness that we are reading an ancient text. But often the traits gesture toward a whole mental world.

Let me return to the white garments and oil from Ecclesiastes 9:8. I have already noted how the transformation of oil on the head into "a splash of cologne" actually substitutes a modern image for the ancient one. But even without such a substitution, simply phrasing matters in a modern idiom can equally place us in a modern American milieu instead of an ancient one: "put on nice clothes / and make yourself look good" (NCV); "dress up, comb your hair, and look your best" (CEV); "don't skimp on colors and scarves" (MESSAGE); "always look happy and cheerful" (GNB). With none of these renditions have we been transported to an ancient world of white garments and oil on the head.

> "A good translation of the New Testament will preserve a sense of historical and cultural distance. It will . . . show [the modern reader] how the gospel of Jesus appeared to a Jew, and not how that Jew would have thought had he been British or American." —Anthony A. Nichols

Ancient cultures had literary conventions of their own, and one of the most prominent in both Old and New Testaments is the fondness of biblical authors for the conjunction *and* as a way of tying events together and achieving fluidity. The result of this stylistic trait is not only a quaint artistry but also a mind-set that differs from the disjointedness that characterizes our own culture.[3] The repeated and formulaic *and* creates a sense of continuity and coherence in regard to events and history. The short, self-contained sentences of some modern Bible translations read like Albert Camus's novel *The Stranger*, where the world dies and is reborn from one sentence to the next.

### Preserving the Words of the Original

I must not leave unstated something that should be obvious but in the current climate is not: it is impossible to be transparent to the original text without translating the actual words of the original text. Much of the mental and social world of biblical authors resides in the words that they use, including idiomatic constructions. Equally, we are unlikely to enter the world of the original text if concrete vocabulary is replaced by abstractions.

> - "It is surely unfortunate to lose the sense of otherness in slicing away Hebrew and Greek vividness." —David Daniell
> - "In general I have always preferred the King James Version simply because it has what seems to me an appropriate flavor of a past time." —Joseph Wood Krutch

For example, the epithet "God of hosts" takes us to the heart of Hebraic conceptions of God's transcendence and of the heavenly realm. The abstraction "God almighty" (NIV) does not open the door that allows us to see those things. The idiomatic formula "he slept with his fathers" conveys much about ancient views of the continuity of generations that the translation "died" does not.

The euphemism "knew" for sexual union captures much of the mystery and profundity of married sexuality and thereby hints at how other eras have viewed the sanctity of marriage. The crass modern "had intercourse" or "had sex" captures none of those things. To retain the original text's statement that believers are "firstfruits" to God (James 1:18) at once provides an entry into how the authors of the New Testament regarded the Christian faith as rooted in Old Testament belief and practice, something that disappears in such translations as "choice possession" (NLT) and "special people" (CEV).

### Summary: Preserving the Original Text

The handful of illustrations that I have supplied will suffice to make the point that modern translations quickly line up on one side of a great divide. Some translations want to make the Bible seem like a modern book. Other translations want to preserve the actual nature of the biblical world. This is not to say that dynamic equivalent translations do not retain much of the atmosphere of the biblical world, though we need to acknowledge a great range in this regard. But *all* dynamic equivalent translators are on the lookout for ways to make the Bible seem modern, and they are quick to stigmatize translations that deviate in any way from modern expressions and customs.

### Why a Translation Should Be Transparent to the Original Text

There are three reasons why the ideal English translation gives readers a direct and unobstructed view of the original text. The first is rooted in the nature of written discourse. The goal of written discourse is to enable a reader to know exactly what the author said as a way of knowing the author's thoughts and feelings. As readers, we want access to the author. I would go so far as to call this the cornerstone of communication theory.

Related to that, an author has the right to set the agenda in regard to (a) what is put before us and (b) how it is expressed. When we read a book that is published in the author's native language, we would regard it as unethical if a publisher were to introduce changes to what the author wrote. We should hold translators to the same standard instead of allowing the translation process to become the occasion for license.

> Dynamic equivalent translations "focus on the reader's subjectivity *as it exists before it encounters the biblical text.* They seem to assume that the text itself has little role in 'creating' its reader, or that readers need to become competent and 'worthy' of the texts they read." —Raymond C. Van Leeuwen (italics in original)

In addition to protecting the rights of an author, essentially literal translations are true to the literal facts of the matter. Getting the literal facts straight is surely the foundation of truth. If the details that would allow us to see the world of the biblical text are removed from our sight, we lack the information that would give us an accurate picture of what actually happens in the Bible and in many instances it represents a falsification of the Bible.

Finally, the ability of the Bible to challenge familiar assumptions and patterns of behavior resides partly in the way in which the biblical world stands over against the modern world and offers an alternative to it. If the Bible is "made over" to appear modern (a stated goal of most dynamic equivalent translators), all that a reader is likely to get from it is a confirmation of existing biases. As one translator puts it, "The danger of [functional equivalent] translations is that they shape the Bible too much to fit our world and our expectations."[4]

One of my former students, who is now a minister, offered the viewpoint that he enjoys reading the New Testament in his preferred essentially literal translation because he "can see the Greek that lies behind it." This is a testimony to the way in which it is transparent to the original text.

# 13

# PRESERVING THE LITERARY
# QUALITIES OF THE BIBLE

A GOOD TRANSLATION preserves the literary qualities that the Bible possesses and in fact exhibits on every page. Despite paying lip service to the literary nature of the Bible, modernizing translations continually violate that very principle. To confuse the contemporary translation scene, other modern translators stigmatize respect for literary principles as being elitist and as producing a translation that phrases things in an "unnatural" way.

## Why the Literary Dimension of the Bible Matters

Preserving the literary qualities of the Bible begins with an acknowledgment that the Bible is overwhelmingly literary in nature. If we are not convinced of that, preserving literary qualities in translation will not be a priority. So let me briefly make the case for the Bible as a literary document.

The most customary way of defining literature is by its genres ("types or kinds of writing"). The two main genres of literature and of the Bible are narrative and poetry, both of which are comprised of numerous subtypes such as hero story, quest story, lament psalm, or nature poem. Other main genres both within the Bible and beyond it are prophecy, satire, visionary writing, drama, oratory, and epistle. Putting all of this together, it is indisputable that in its external format the Bible is a literary anthology.

Second, literature is characterized by taking human experience as its subject. This is in contrast to expository writing, which takes ideas, facts, and summary of information as its subject. The Bible does, indeed, contain expository writing, but such writing does not dominate. Wherever the Bible is literary, it advertises that fact by "showing" rather than "telling"—by presenting characters in action or poetic images and metaphors.

> "There is . . . a sense in which the Bible, since it is after all literature, cannot properly be read except as literature; and the different parts of it as the different sorts of literature they are." —C. S. Lewis

Third, literary writing is overtly artistic in a way that expository writing is not. Good expository writing is transparent in the sense that the style and medium do not draw attention to themselves. By contrast, literary writing *does* draw attention to itself. One writer in the Bible gives us his philosophy and methodology of writing, and it turns out to be a thoroughly literary version of those things: "Besides being wise, the Preacher also taught the people knowledge, weighing and studying and arranging many proverbs with great care. The Preacher sought to find words of delight" (Eccl. 12:9–10, ESV). Here we find a picture of the author as conscious artist, selecting and arranging with great care, as well as a wordsmith who loves beautiful words.

The foregoing comments do not by themselves move us into the subject of the right kind of English Bible translation. They are a foundation on which I will build the case for preserving the literary qualities of the original. My claim is that a translation is adequate only if it respects the literary nature of the Bible.

In earlier parts of this book I covered two topics that relate to the subject of this chapter, and I will not repeat that material here. The primary points of those topics, though, need to be restated in the context of the literary dimension of the Bible. The two points are as follows:

- Literature is concrete rather than abstract. Dynamic equivalent translations show a readiness to replace concrete words with abstract ones because of the translators' preoccupation with interpreting the meanings of the text for modern readers.

- Literature does not generally sound like everyday oral conversation. It possesses qualities that raise it above that level of vocabulary and syntax. Colloquializing translations consistently lower the Bible from a literary style to the level of nonliterary, informal everyday *oral* discourse. (I have stressed the concept of orality to draw attention to the fact that colloquial Bible translations are pitched considerably lower than the level of writing at which educated people operate most of the time.)

## Respecting an Author's Literary Intention

No hermeneutical principle has been more dominant in evangelical circles than the idea of authorial intention. According to this principle, we need to interpret a statement in keeping with what we know or infer about the author's intention in making the statement. But dynamic equivalent and essentially literal translators do not agree on how to apply this principle.

Dynamic equivalent translators believe that they are being true to an author's intention when they interpret the meaning of a statement even while departing from what the author said. For example, in Psalm 91:1 the poet begins his poem with the clause, "He who dwells in the shelter of the Most High" (ESV, NASB, NIV; NLT nearly identical). Here are three dynamic equivalent translations that show the bias of that translation philosophy by removing the metaphor of dwelling in a shelter: "under the protection of" (CEV); "whoever goes to the Lord for safety" (GNB); "sit down in the High God's presence" (MESSAGE).

When challenged on this maneuver of replacing the metaphor of dwelling in the shelter with such abstractions as "protection," "safety," and "presence," dynamic equivalent translators regularly claim that they have been faithful to the author's *meaning*, if not to his words. The preface to the NLT is explicit about this viewpoint: by transposing the Old Testament metaphor "slept with his fathers" to "died," the translators have given "*the real meaning*" of the original, and by replacing a metaphor with an abstract interpretation the translators have made "*the meaning immediately clear*" (italics added).

But wait a minute: surely it is a natural premise that what writers *mean* to say is what they *say*. Similarly with the concept of *intention*: essentially literal translators assume that what writers intended to say is *what they did say*. We ourselves would protest if someone were to claim to know better than we do "what we meant" or "what we intended."

> When translators change what an author wrote to make it match their own understanding of the author's statement, they in effect adopt the principle that readers determine meaning. E. D. Hirsch has championed the opposite viewpoint that authors determine meaning: a written text has "to represent *somebody's* meaning—if not the author's, then the [interpreter's]. . . . Validity [in interpretation] requires a norm—a meaning that is stable and determinate no matter how broad its range of implication and application. A stable and determinate meaning requires an author's determining will. . . . All valid interpretation of every sort is founded on the re-cognition of what an author meant."

Replacing the statement of a biblical author with something else is one way in which dynamic equivalent translators claim to convey what the author allegedly meant or intended; the other common ploy is to add interpretive commentary to the translation. "Your neck is like the tower of David," the poet states in Song of Solomon 4:4 (NIV, NASB, NKJV, ESV). Dynamic equivalent translations operate on the premise that this does not adequately express the author's intended meaning, so they massage the statement:

"Your neck is *as stately as* the tower of David" (NLT); "your neck is *as beautiful as* the tower of David" (NLT, 2004); "your neck is *more graceful than* the tower of David" (CEV); "the smooth, lithe lines of your neck command notice" (MESSAGE).

The essential principle, regularly violated by some translation committees, is this: when authors embody their message in a literary form such as metaphor, *they intend to entrust their utterance to ordinary methods of literary interpretation.* That is their intention. To respect authorial intention is to leave the statements of the author in their composed form. If that form is literary in nature, the literary properties of the text are what the author intends us to have at our disposal.

## Multilayered Discourse

Another quality of literary writing is that it is often so compact and skillfully constructed that it says more than one thing at the same time. The literary term for this is *ambiguity*, which literary authors and literary critics regard as a virtue. For these people, ambiguity implies not only the phenomenon of multiple meanings but also the possibility of an accompanying elusive and mysterious quality, such as we find in some of Jesus' "hard sayings."

Essentially literal translations retain the ambiguity that the original text possesses, while the general drift of dynamic equivalent translators is to be nervous about it and replace it with a single preferred interpretation. Since my procedure in this book is to illustrate the issues that I raise but not exhaustively demonstrate the extent to which the two kinds of translation do various things, I have chosen just one passage with which to compare translations in regard to multilayered discourse.

The last line of Psalm 88 clarifies the issues nicely. The original states, "My companions have become darkness" (ESV), or (even more cursory) "My acquaintances—darkness" (Weiser).[1] Certainly the line requires pondering and analysis. Several readings are simultaneously possible: (1) the speaker's friends have vanished and are as absent or invisible as darkness; (2) the ignominious desertion by the speaker's friends makes them morally dark—people with a dark stain on them because of their behavior; (3) darkness is the speaker's friend or acquaintance. Since biblical scholars and translators have considered the original to be problematical, I should add that as a literary critic I find the line rich in ambiguity of the type I regularly encounter in poetry. I am not bothered by it in the least.

Translators who dislike ambiguity have done a number of things with the last line of Psalm 88, a variability that already signals the problems that arise when literary ambiguity is compromised, namely, the inability of dynamic equivalent translators to agree among themselves. Three translations choose the meaning that the speaker's companions are "in darkness" (RSV, NASB, NRSV), a statement that is as elusive as the untouched original. "Only darkness remains," says another translation (NLT), which removes the friends from the utterance even though they are present in the original and which narrows the range of possible meanings to one. Other translations reverse the word order of the sentence and change the plural reference to singular: "Darkness is now my only companion" (REB) or "The darkness is my closest friend" (NIV). The latter are defensible readings, but (a) they are only one of several options, and (b) because they reverse the word order of the original and change the number from plural to singular, they are the least likely of the legitimate options.

---

- "Ambiguity, arresting imagery, and the evocation of multiple associations pervade the Bible. Jesus himself often used such language to shock or puzzle the hearer, to force him to introspect, or to look at things in a completely new way. The substitution of paraphrase for metaphor always involves loss of meaning." —Anthony C. Nichols
- "In [the King James translators'] view the translator's task was not to assume that there is one clear meaning to which the text should be reduced, but instead to open out the text to include as much as possible."—Gerald Hammond

---

What the translators' toils over the last line of Psalm 88 show is that uneasiness over ambiguity is usually both unnecessary and impoverishing to the meaning of the text. Some of the translations that smooth out the last line of Psalm 88 are more immediately understandable than the untouched line, but they are also reductionistic and lose the multidimensional quality and mystery of the original. One of the points elaborated in A. H. Nichols's critique of dynamic equivalent translations is that "the commitment to explicitness means that the metaphor and the motifs of the Bible had to be reprocessed and replaced by the explicit, analytical language with which Westerners feel more comfortable," a process that "always involves loss of meaning."[2]

I need to add that dynamic equivalent translators generally do not deny that ambiguity and multiple meanings exist in the original. They do not approve of that situation, however, so they interpose their preferred interpretation and shield readers from the ambiguities of the original. It is just another instance of dynamic equivalent translators operating on the premise that the Bible needs to be corrected and that modern translators can improve what the biblical authors gave us.

## Preserving Mystery and Subtlety

A related quality of good translation is preservation of the mystery that great literature possesses and that sacred books possess in abundance. Additionally, literature achieves many of its effects by a certain subtlety and indirection. On this issue, too, the rival translation philosophies operate in generally antithetical ways. Essentially literal translations pass on whatever the original possesses, while dynamic equivalent translation is a grand exercise in Spelling It Out.

Proof of this divergence exists on nearly every page of the Bible. "He leads me beside still waters," Psalm 23:2 states. Psalm 23 is a pastoral (shepherd's) poem built around the motif of an ideal day in the shepherd's life. The opening picture of green pastures and still waters evokes a familiar detail of shepherding in ancient Palestine—the resting of the sheep for several hours at midday in a type of oasis. The poet expects readers to know this daily routine of a shepherd's life without explaining it. Not content with the simple statement phrase "beside still waters," the urge to Spell It Out yields the translation, "He leads me to water *where I may rest*" (REB; italics show what has been added to the original).

---

- "Literature, and especially religious literature, is not primarily concerned with being clear and reasonable; it is connotative rather than direct, suggestive rather than explicit." —Dwight Macdonald
- "Another quality that can fairly be demanded of a Bible is mystery, much of which evaporates in the prosiness [of modern translations]."—Stanley Edgar Hyman
- "In the name of fashionable communications-theory, slicing away metaphors in English removes the potential for mystery which is at the heart of what is meant by the Holy." —David Daniell

---

Even turning a metaphor into a simile (using the formula *like* or *as*) is a way of undermining the subtlety and indirection of the original. "The LORD God is a sun and shield," Psalm 84:11 simply says in essentially literal translations. The poetic compactness of the statement is eroded in the following prose-like translation:

> Our LORD and our God,
> you are like the sun
> and also like a shield. (CEV)

"The lines have fallen for me in pleasant places," Psalm 16:6 states. This allusion to the dividing of the Promised Land into portions is a hugely evocative statement, made even more powerful by its succinctness and refusal to spell out what lines are in view. Dynamic equivalent translators are nervous about those very qualities, so they tug at the verse until the impact of the original is compromised and finally evaporates: "the boundary lines have fallen for me in pleasant places" (NIV, NRSV); "the land you have given me is a pleasant land" (NLT); "you make my life pleasant" (CEV); "how wonderful are your gifts to me, / how good they are" (GNB).

As we move down the line with those renditions, we lose a great deal more than indirection and subtlety. We finally lose the literal text entirely, with the "lines" dropping out of sight. This is hardly surprising: dynamic equivalence is founded on the premises of a reader of whom little can be expected and a text that needs to be corrected. By contrast, in preserving the succinctness and indirection of the original text, a good translation also embodies a certain mystery that is appropriate to a sacred book.

## Translating the Poetry of the Bible

At least a third of the Bible is poetry. Figurative language appears abundantly in the non-poetic parts of the Bible as well, most notably in the discourses of Jesus, the Epistles, and the book of Revelation. Accordingly, any discussion of the literary aspect of Bible translation necessarily involves a consideration of how poetry fares in a given translation.

Poets speak a language all their own. The image is the primary ingredient in poetry (an image is any word that names a concrete action or thing, such as "running" and "water"). Many of the images of poetry are comparisons in the form of metaphor and simile. Additional figures of speech like personification, metonymy, and synecdoche round out the poet's repertoire.

English translations of the Bible show a wide range of fidelity to or departure from the poetic idiom of the Bible. In the very nature of the case, essentially literal translations preserve the poetry of the Bible because the translators have retained the actual words of the original. By contrast, dynamic equivalent translations give us only some of the poetic idiom of biblical authors; much of the time they substitute an abstraction for the concreteness of the original. As a way of highlighting the differences, I have chosen as examples the following passages in which the two types of translations either retain or discard the poetic idiom of biblical authors.

A master image in the Old Testament is "the hand of God." For example, Job tells his counselors at one point, "I will teach you concerning the hand of God" (Job 27:11, ESV; NKJV nearly identical). Dynamic equivalent translators do not have preservation of the poetry of the Bible as a priority, so they remove the image of God's hand and render it as an abstraction: "power of God" (NIV), or "God's power" (NEB, REB, GNB, HCSB, NLT).

In the haunting portrait of the physiological symptoms of old age that concludes the book of Ecclesiastes, the poet asserts that "the almond tree blossoms" (Eccl. 12:5). The poet trusted his readers to interpret the metaphor of the blossoming almond tree as a picture of white hair. But when translators begin with the premise that readers cannot interpret poetry, they either substitute an abstraction for the blossoming almond tree or add commentary that loses the punch and subtlety of the original metaphor: "your hair will turn white" (GNB); "your hair will turn as white as almond blossoms" (CEV); "white-haired and withered" (NLT).

> "Biblical metaphors drop into our hearts like a seed in soil and make us think, precisely because they are not obvious at first. The translator who removes biblical metaphors to make the text 'easier' for readers may defeat the purpose of the Holy Spirit, who chose a metaphor in the first place. Metaphors grab us and work on us and in us. . . . The abandonment of basic biblical metaphors in many translations follows naturally from [functional equivalence] theory, because the target audiences may not use such expressions. But it is the foreignness of metaphors that is their virtue. Metaphors make us stop and think, Now what does that mean?" —Raymond C. Van Leeuwen

Psalm 73 includes a vivid poetic portrait of the prosperous wicked. The poet first compares them to animals that have all the food they need: "for they have no pangs until death; / their bodies are fat and sleek" (Ps. 73:4, ESV). A good literary translation retains the poetry of the original; an unliterary translation turns the poetry into abstraction. In the NIV, the pangs become "struggles," and the phrase "fat and sleek" becomes the abstract "healthy and strong." The NLT also has "healthy and strong," and additionally substitutes "live such a painless life" for the picture of having no pangs. Other translations change the image of "no pangs until death" to the abstractions "they have an easy time until they die" (HCSB) and "they never have to suffer" (CEV).

There is no need to belabor this point. Dynamic equivalent proponents and prefaces are forthright about the matter. The preface to the NLT states, "Metaphorical language is often difficult for contemporary readers to understand, so at times we have chosen to . . . illuminate the metaphor." Eugene Nida enthusiastically endorsed the Good News Bible's removal of metaphors from Psalm 1:1 on the ground that "many present-day readers" find the metaphors "strange," with the result that removing the metaphors makes the verse "so much clearer."[3]

With statements like these we are right at the heart of the dynamic equivalent view of the Bible as a deficient book in which the authors miscalculated what readers can handle. We can never remind ourselves too often that the biblical authors had the lexical resources to express their content as modern translators render it. They could have said "power of God" instead of "arm of God," but under the inspiration of the Holy Spirit they said what they said.

## Chapter Summary

If "all Scripture is breathed out by God" (2 Tim. 3:16), we have no alternative but to conclude that God gave us the Bible that he wanted us to have. Dynamic equivalent translators do not believe it in actual practice. They apologize for statements in the original that "have little meaning" for "most readers today" (NIV preface), or references to ancient customs that "are meaningless to most people" (NCV preface), or metaphorical language that "is often quite difficult for contemporary readers to understand" (NLT preface). Dynamic equivalent translators keep "correcting" the Bible for its deficiencies, including its literary style and vocabulary.

Essentially literal translators accept the Bible as it was written. This leads them to embrace the literary forms of the Bible and strive to preserve them in an English translation. They translate in keeping with the authors' literary intentions, allow multilayered statements their full range of meanings, attempt to preserve the mystery of the Bible where it exists, and retain the poetry of the original within the changes that translation always requires.

---

# PART FIVE

# The Bible in the Church

Even though the prefaces to dynamic equivalent translations sometimes signal the translators' awareness that the Bible is a book that exists for the church and not just for individuals, at its very core the dynamic equivalence movement is aimed at the individual Bible reader. The preoccupation with making the translation immediately understandable presupposes an individual's sitting down and reading the Bible alone, without a preacher or teacher present to explain the text. The preface of one dynamic equivalent Bible comes right out and asserts that it is aimed partly at "those who have never read the Bible" (SEB).

In this concluding part of my book, I take up the public, congregational aspect of Bible translation. In doing so, I will cover territory that is often neglected in the current Bible translation debate.

# 14

# ORAL READING OF THE BIBLE

WHEN THE NIV originally swept the evangelical world, the Bible-reading public did not have a clue as to what was happening. All that most people knew is that the church needed a modern-language translation. The new translation philosophy that underlay the NIV and the contemporaneous Good News Bible was knowledge limited to a relatively small circle of people, mainly scholars and professional Bible translators. Only much later did the evangelical world at large become attuned to what had happened on the translation scene.

On one point, though, laypeople *did* know what was happening from the start. Loosely speaking, they knew that when the Bible was read orally it did not "sound right." Since the more extreme forms of colloquializing entered the scene later, that could not have been the trigger to this awareness. Instead it was the rhythm of the new translations, and when supplied with the formula *staccato effect*, the average person knew at least one point on which the new translations were deficient.

## Understanding Rhythm

I need to counteract a possible misconception right at the outset: an exploration of the rhythm of an English Bible translation necessarily involves the use of technical terms, but we should not therefore conclude that the matter is of interest only to a handful of literary scholars. On the contrary, rhythm is one of the most important criteria for a book that is read aloud. Good rhythm in a Bible translation is like a qualifying exam: if a translation cannot measure up in this area, it is not in the running to be a superior Bible for public use or even for oral reading in smaller groups.

## The Elements of Rhythm

Rhythm is the regular recurrence of a pattern of sound. When the medium is language (as distinct from music), rhythm refers to the flow of words and phrases. The goal of rhythm is smoothness—not a monotonously regular flow, but a flow that is *predominantly* regular. The very word *rhythm* implies a back-and-forth recurrence, the rise and fall of language. Anything that impedes the smoothness of the flow is detrimental to good rhythm.

The test of rhythm is simply to read passages aloud. No formal analysis is needed to distinguish good rhythm from inferior rhythm, though it is possible for people to become so accustomed to bad rhythm that they lose their ear for good rhythm. If in oral reading a passage ebbs and flows smoothly, avoids abrupt stops between words and phrases where possible, and provides a sense of continuity, it is rhythmically excellent. If a translation bumps along, impedes the flow of language, and is consistently staccato in effect, it is rhythmically inferior.

## The King James Version: The Gold Standard

I do not have leisure to explain what makes the King James translation the best English Bible in its rhythm, but we should give credit where credit is due. The KJV is incomparably the best English translation in regard to rhythm.

154

> - "The King James [translators] had ears. . . . They were more sensitive to speech rhythms and more practiced in them, far better trained in rhetoric and respectful of it, than their modern successors." —Craig Thompson
> - "The heart of this richness and resonance [of the KJV] is the musicality of the Jacobean Translators' work. . . . [Their] consistent attention to a grand and heavily musical rhythm" is the vehicle by which a "majesty is infused into the body of the text."—Adam Nicolson

While we have lost some of the resources that the King James translators had at their disposal (such as unaccented inflectional -*eth* suffixes to keep the rhythm flowing, as in "runneth"), it is nonetheless possible for modern translations to approximate the rhythmic excellence of the King James translation if the translators are willing to be influenced by the gold standard represented by the KJV.

### Poetic Rhythm

Even though Hebrew poetry was not based on regular meter as English poetry is, and even though we read it in translation, nonetheless rhythm is a larger consideration with the poetry of the Bible than with its prose. This is the case because the recurrent unit in poetry is the line, a shorter and more repetitive unit than the sentence, which is the recurrent element in prose. Additionally, emotionally charged language tends to be rhythmic, and poetry is preeminently the language of emotion.

For purposes of illustration, I have selected specimen verses from the psalms that highlight the issues. As printed below, the syllables in capitals are accented syllables. The vertical lines divide the material into rhythmic feet (the individual rhythmic unit in a poetic line). To demonstrate what flows well and what is disjointed, we need to read the passages aloud. In the discussion that follows, I will give examples of rhythmic excellence and rhythmic failure.

## Psalm 24:1

The KJV almost always sets the standard of excellence in regard to rhythm. Here is how it renders Psalm 24:1:

> The EARTH | is the LORD'S | and the FULness | thereOF;
> the WORLD, | and THEY | that DWELL | thereIN.

The meter flows regularly and smoothly. The RSV and ESV give us the rhythmic equivalent of the KJV, showing that a translation can update vocabulary without abandoning the KJV rhythm:

> The EARTH | is the LORD'S | and the FULness | thereOF;
> The WORLD | and THOSE | who DWELL | thereIN.

The NEB likewise fares well with this verse:

> The EARTH | is the LORD'S | and ALL | that is | IN IT,
> the WORLD | and THOSE | who DWELL | thereIN.

The first line ends with a jolting, staccato effect, but otherwise the two lines flow well.

This changes when we come to most dynamic equivalent translations of the verse. Here is the NRSV rendition:

> The EARTH | is the LORD'S | and ALL | that is | IN IT,
> the WORLD, | and THOSE | who LIVE | IN IT.

Both lines end with a staccato effect. The NIV has the same jolting effect at the ends of the lines:

> The EARTH | is the LORD'S, | and EVerything | IN IT,
> the WORLD, | and ALL | who LIVE | IN IT.

The ends of the lines break the back of the rhythm.

Other translations produce additional rhythmic deficiencies with Psalm 24:1. The NASB yields this infelicity:

> The EARTH | is the LORD'S, | and ALL | IT | conTAINS,
> The WORLD, | and THOSE | who DWELL | IN IT.

Again, the lines begin well and end with broken rhythm in the second half. The REB is similar in its difficulties:

To the LORD | beLONG | the EARTH | and EVerything | IN IT,
The WORLD | and ALL | ITS | inHABitants.

Here the rhythm breaks down into staccato effect at various points in both lines.

> "The language of elevated thought or feeling is always rhythmic. Strong feeling of whatever sort . . . imposes on speech a rhythmic beat. . . . Now the Biblical literature, to an almost unrivalled degree, is profoundly tinged with feeling. . . . No literature, I think, is so pervaded with profound and passionate emotion as the writings of the Old and the New Testaments."
> —John Livingston Lowes

## Psalm 48:1

The NKJV, RSV, NASB, and ESV are in agreement in regard to the opening verse of Psalm 48. They translate it thus:

GREAT | is the LORD | and GREATly | to be PRAISED.

The rhythm flows smoothly, beginning with an accented syllable (a common occurrence at the beginning of a poetic line) and then maintaining the momentum with a good intermixture of unaccented syllables followed by accented ones. There is a nice balance between the two halves of the line, each ending with an anapestic foot (two unaccented syllables followed by an accented syllable). Furthermore, both halves begin by accentuating the key word *great/greatly*.

The NEB rearranges the elements of the sentence from the previous translations, but it flows well:

The LORD | is GREAT | and WORTHy | of our PRAISE.

This is the rhythmic equivalent of the previous rendition, except for the opening two iambic feet.

The story is otherwise in the NIV and REB versions:

GREAT | is the LORD | and MOST | WORTHy | of PRAISE.

The flow breaks down halfway through the line with the jux-
taposition of two accented syllables at the end and beginning
of a poetic foot, though the line recovers at the end. (The word
*most* needs to be emphasized because its denotative function is
to emphasize the adjective [*worthy*] that it modifies; if we do not
emphasize it, it is a mere filler word, something that its meaning
and intensive function do not allow.)

### Further Specimens

In the following sequence of paired items, I have again chosen
examples that highlight the differences between good and bad
rhythm. Psalm 104:33 flows beautifully in the following translation of it:

I will SING | to the LORD | as LONG | as I [unaccented] LIVE.
(RSV, NKJV, NLT, ESV)

The key to the success of this line is the predominant anapestic
meter (two unaccented syllables followed by an accented syllable).
In the following version, the four consecutive accented syllables
at the end of the line bog down the flow:

I will SING | to the LORD | ALL MY LIFE. (NIV)

Psalm 1:3 unfolds in three rhythmic waves in the following
version:

In ALL | that he DOES, | he PROSpers. (RSV, NEB, ESV)

The following rendition is staccato in effect:

WhatEVer | he DOES | PROSpers. (NIV)

Similarly, the following line is staccato in the first half and too
loaded with successive unaccented syllables in the second half:

158

THOSE PEOple | sucCEED | in EVerything | they DO. (CEV)

For those of my readers who find this discussion rather technical, let me say again that the test of rhythm is one that anyone can perform without using technical analysis. That test is simply to read the passages aloud. My analysis simply explains *why* we respond to each rendition as we do.

## Prose Rhythm

Prose rhythm is different from poetic rhythm because the recurrent unit is the sentence instead of the line. Poetic feet give way to larger syntactic units, and phraseology (the arrangement of material into phrases as opposed to poetic feet) counts for more than with poetry as the unit that provides the flow of the utterance. Having noted these differences, though, we need to look for the same thing in prose as in poetry—a smooth, wavelike recurrence, a rise and fall in the movement of language. The technical term for this is *cadence*.

## 1 Corinthians 13:4, 7, 8

For an example of oratorical prose at its most formal, it is hard to beat 1 Corinthians 13, an encomium in praise of love. The following translation moves in a smooth flow of rising and falling cadence:

> Love is patient and kind; love does not envy or boast. . . . Love bears all things, believes all things, hopes all things, endures all things. Love never ends. (ESV)

Someone reading that passage from the pulpit or in a small group Bible study will feel a sense of excellence in uttering the statement. That is decidedly untrue of the following two brusque renditions of the same passage:

> Love is patient, love is kind. It does not envy, it does not boast, it is not proud. . . . It always protects, always trusts, always hopes, always perseveres. Love never fails. (NIV)

Love is kind and patient, never jealous, boastful, proud, or rude. . . . Love is always supportive, loyal, hopeful, and trusting. Love never fails! (CEV)

These two translations do not read gracefully. Much of the beauty of the original vanishes with them. They dispense information in utilitarian fashion but are not winsome and meditative, as the first version is.

## Why Good Rhythm Matters

Why is excellence of rhythm important? One answer is aesthetic: good rhythm is beautiful, and bad rhythm is grating and offputting in its unattractiveness. Beauty matters to God, who is its source. If beauty matters to God, it should matter to those who produce and read Bible translations. Literary critic H. L. Mencken, an outspoken non-Christian, called the King James Bible "unquestionably the most beautiful book the world."[1] It should be more but not *less* than the most beautiful book in the world for Christians as well, and rhythm is one factor among several that can make it such.

> A Bible translation read in churches needs to appeal to "the auditory imagination," a "feeling for syllable and rhythm, penetrating far below the conscious levels of thought and feeling, invigorating every word." —T. S. Eliot

Second, good rhythm is essential to any text that is uttered orally. The Bible is preeminently an oral book, read aloud in public worship, on ceremonial occasions, and around the table. Dwight Macdonald has written about modern translations, "The most damaging effect of modernizing the usage is the alteration of rhythm, which is all-important in a book so often read aloud; quite aside from literary grace, the ceremonial effect of the Bible is enhanced by the interesting, varied, and suitable rhythms of K.J.V."[2]

Third, rhythm is an aid to memory as well as to oral performance. A line that flows smoothly is easier to memorize than a line that bumps along and impedes the flow of thought. Good rhythm is often aphoristic in effect. Literary critic F. L. Lucas, in lamenting what modern translations have done with the King James rendition, "Come unto me, all ye that labour and are heavy laden, and I will give you rest," comments that modernization "ruins the beauty of rhythm which has helped the memories of generations, and *kept the Bible running in their heads*" (italics added to call attention to what is often overlooked).[3]

Finally, rhythm is the natural concomitant of impassioned and heightened speech and writing. Earlier I quoted John Livingston Lowes on how "the language of elevated thought and feeling is always rhythmic," and how the Bible "is profoundly tinged with feeling."[4] The decline in rhythmic excellence and the decline in elevated feeling have gone hand-in-hand in most modern translations, and it is hard to know what is cause and what is effect. Dorothy Thompson has written, "Apart from musical accompaniment, this matter of beat, cadence, the rise and fall of sentences, is part of the magic of poetry and prose, contributing to its evocative character, its overtones and undertones, its symphonic style, which greatly distinguishes the familiar Bible [the KJV]."[5]

### Summary: Rhythm

Considerations of rhythm are important in English Bible translation. For a book that is read aloud as often as the Bible is, excellent rhythm should not be regarded as optional but as essential. Translators who ignore it pay the inevitable price: the absence of smooth rhythm advertises itself the moment we hear the Bible read orally, and the Bible at once becomes a diminished book.

Modern translators are quick to claim that their translations are ideally suited to public reading, but most of the claims are demonstrably false. The loss to Bible readers and Christian worship has been immense.

# 15

# THE NEED FOR A TRANSLATION
# THAT PEOPLE CAN TRUST
# AND RESPECT

ONE OF THE MOST salient traits of the current evangelical scene is the eclipse of the Bible—from pulpits, in small groups and Sunday school classes, in people's reading habits. Biblical illiteracy is the inevitable result of this eclipse and is a well-documented phenomenon.[1] A Yale University professor looked back on his career of teaching and concluded, "When I arrived at Yale, even those who came from nonreligious backgrounds knew the Bible better than most of those now who come from churchgoing families."[2]

Modern translations play a role in this cultural drift, though I make no claim to be able to prove what is cause and what is effect. My subject in this part of the book is the ideal Bible translation. In this chapter I will argue that the church needs a Bible that has stature and authority and that therefore commands respect. Such an ideal necessarily exists in a contemporary context, so once again I will find it necessary to set the ideal in contrast to its opposite.

## A Stable Bible

Before the arrival of dynamic equivalence on the translation scene, the variability among English Bible translations was within the normal range of lexical tolerance. No one thought much about variations among translations because translators operated on the shared premise that the goal of translation was to find the English words or phrases that best expressed the meanings of the words of the original text. Additionally, as I showed in my history of English Bible translation in the early chapters of this book, translators viewed their task as building upon and refining the long tradition of English Bible translation, as opposed to seeing how novel they could be in producing a Bible that was unlike its predecessors.

The syndrome of the destabilized Bible has followed in the wake of the dynamic equivalent movement. By destabilization I mean the phenomenon of wide variation in how the same verse of the Bible is translated. The original text cannot possibly mean all that modern translations have given us, with the result that we are left in uncertainty about what the Bible says. Before long, people give up the quest to know what the Bible says.

### John 6:27

Here is how three essentially literal translations render the conclusion of John 6:27:

- ". . . for on Him the Father, even God, has set His seal." (NASB)
- ". . . because God the Father has set His seal on Him." (NKJV)
- "For on him God the Father has set his seal." (ESV)

164

This is a stable text. The key phrase "has set his seal" is present in all three translations. This stability is lost in the following five dynamic equivalent translations of the same passage:

- "On him God the Father has placed his seal of approval." (NIV, TNIV)
- ". . . for on him God the Father has set the seal of his authority." (REB)
- ". . . because God the Father has given him the right to do so." (CEV)
- "For God the Father has sent me for that very purpose." (NLT)
- "He and what he does are guaranteed by God the Father to last." (MESSAGE)

This is a destabilized text. An English reader has no way of knowing whether the word *seal* appears in the original. If it does appear, is it a seal of approval or a seal of authority? The words *right, purpose,* and *guarantee* in the last three translations are definitely not identical. So what does the passage say? The dynamic equivalent translations confuse us rather than inform us. If we do not know what the Bible actually says, we cannot elevate it to the status of an authority even if we might wish to do so.

---

In *The NIV Reconsidered*, a book that is critical of modern trends in Bible translation, authors Earl Radmacher and Zane C. Hodges identify "five present-day problems" as follows: (1) decreasing confidence in the inspired text; (2) decreasing basis for correct interpretation; (3) decreasing use of Scripture in the worship service; (4) decreasing expository preaching from the Bible; (5) decreasing memorization of Scripture.

---

## Psalm 73:7

In the portrait of the prosperous wicked that the poet paints in Psalm 73, the portrait has a double thrust. Ostensibly the poet says that he envied the wicked, but other details in the portrait subvert or deconstruct that claim. A prime example is the first line of verse 7, which essentially literal translations handle this way:

- "Their eyes stand out with fatness." (KJV)
- "Their eye bulges from fatness." (NASB)
- "Their eyes swell out through fatness." (ESV)

This is a stable text. In keeping with the technique used in the rest of the portrait, the three translations are in agreement that the poet is directing our attention to a body part. Additionally, they all agree that the person being described is fat. The variability among *stand out, bulges,* and *swell out* is the normal variability that exists when translators determine the most precise word that matches the original. There is an element of visual grotesqueness in the portrait, though on the other side of the equation lies the fact that in order to be that fat a person needed to be wealthy enough to afford as much food as he wanted.

The consensus breaks down when dynamic equivalent translators ply their trade with the line:

- "From their callous hearts comes iniquity." (NIV)
- "These fat cats have everything." (NLT)
- "Their hearts pour out evil." (GNB)
- "Their spite oozes like fat." (JB)
- "Pampered and overfed. . ." (MESSAGE)
- "They are looking for profits." (NCV)

This is perplexing in the extreme. Does the poet name a body part or not? If so, is it the heart rather than the eye? Does the poet use the image of cats? If so, how could essentially literal translators have missed it? Does the poet name "spite," specifically? Does the poet use the financial language of "profits?"

After pondering all of those questions, the final questions readily become, who can know? And second, who cares? After all, each one of these translations is favored by some people, so surely one is as good as the other, isn't it? Dynamic equivalent translators hope that you read only their preferred rendition. If that is all the data we have on the table, it of course seems plausible. But if we take the time to compare that one translation with what the original says, and then when we check what four or five other dynamic equivalent translations say, often (not always) we are left without certainty as to what the original author actually wrote.

## Summary: A Stable Bible

For the Bible to be central in the life of an individual or church, we need certainty as to what the Bible says. If we lack that certainty, the Bible becomes demoted. Inevitably the mind-set settles in that the Bible might say this or might say that, so let's not put too much confidence in the Bible that we hold in our hands. After all, the person seated next to us at church has a translation that says something different.

## Exaltation and Affective Power

The King James Bible is probably the most exalted book in the English language. All the praises heaped on it for its affective power are warranted. Anyone who still reads the KJV or who can remember a church culture where the KJV was used knows what it feels like to have a Bible with power. To anyone with normal linguistic sensitivity, the King James Bible possesses authority and commands reverence.

> "One of the King James Bible's most consistent driving forces is the idea of majesty. Its method and its voice are . . . regal. . . . Its qualities are those of grace, stateliness, scale, power. There is no desire to please here; only a belief in the enormous and overwhelming divine authority." —Adam Nicolson

The modern era does not like exaltation and formality of expression. It is generally unaccustomed to a quality expressed by the Latin word *gravitas*—weightiness of content and style. Additionally, as a culture we have settled for light rather than profound emotions; our preferred adjective is "cool" or a trivialized "awesome." Modern colloquializing translations cater to the modern taste, and the result is once again a demotion of the stature of the Bible. To elicit respect, a Bible needs to have the qualities that command such respect.

To illustrate, I will again compare how translations in the King James tradition render a given verse and how a range of modern translations render it.

### Revelation 3:20

One of the most awe-inspiring verses in the whole Bible in the King James tradition is Revelation 3:20: "Behold, I stand at the door and knock" (KJV, NKJV, RSV, NASB, ESV). Colloquializing translations lower the voltage. The NIV reads, "Here I am! I stand at the door and knock." I must acknowledge that the moment I read that statement the picture that ran through my mind was that of the neighborhood brat spoiling a Sunday afternoon nap.

The REB reads, "Here I stand knocking at the door." What comes into my mind is that the person knocking wonders in perplexity why he is doing it. When I read, "Listen! I am standing and knocking at your door" (CEV), I hear the person saying, "I *know* that somebody is home." And a note of irritation enters my mind when I read, "Look, I am standing at the door, knocking" (JB).

### Lowering the Voltage

Modern translations are often an exercise in lowering the emotional and linguistic voltage of the King James tradition. In the grand style, the pen of the ready scribe in Psalm 45:1 "overflows with a goodly theme" (RSV, NRSV; similar in NASB and ESV). In the prosaic tradition, the scribe's heart is merely "stirred" (NIV, NEB, JB). Ho-hum. Other translations transmute the exalted poetry of the utterance into flat prose: "my thoughts are filled with beautiful words" (CEV); "my heart bursts its banks, spilling beauty and

168

goodness" (MESSAGE); "beautiful words fill my mind" (NCV). A "beautiful words" moment—nothing more.

One of Jesus' most evocative aphorisms is Matthew 6:28: "Consider the lilies of the field, how they grow" (KJV, NKJV, ESV). When I unpack that statement in my literature classes, the meanings keep expanding: it is a call to contemplation, observation, meditation, an aesthetic encounter with beauty, introspection, a wise passiveness as we let the observation of nature sink in and affect us. The prosaic substitutes generally dissipate those effects: "see how the lilies of the field grow" (NIV); "think how the flowers grow" (NLV); "look how the wild flowers grow" (CEV); "look at the lilies and how they grow" (NLT); "walk out into the fields and look at the wildflowers" (MESSAGE). A "let's look at the flowers" moment—nothing more.

---

- "The religious passion of Jesus and Paul, transcending modern experience, needs an exalted idiom to be adequately conveyed." —Dwight Macdonald
- "In all languages I know of it has been the universal tendency to express the central ideas of religion in a language more dignified, more archaic even, and with more implicit levels of meaning than that used for the doings of ordinary life." —C. L. Wrenn
- "The Biblical style is eloquent and almost unequaled in emotional expressiveness." —Henry Seidel Canby

---

One of the most profound statements in the Bible is John 14:1: "Let not your hearts be troubled" (nearly all translations). But in a day that seeks novelty and the mundane, if we consult enough dynamic equivalent translations we will find the passage stripped of its profundity: "do not be worried and upset" (GNB);[3] "set your troubled hearts at rest" (NEB, REB); "don't let this throw you" (MESSAGE).

### Summary: Exaltation and Affective Power

As noted previously, Billy Graham said that "it is thrilling to read the Word . . . [in] a style that reads much like today's

169

newspaper."[4] It may be novel, but thrilling is exactly what it is *not*. More importantly, if the Bible is made to sound like the newspaper, that is the level of respect that people will come to accord it. A sacred book should sound like a sacred book. If it does, it will assume the stature of a sacred book in the life of the church and for individuals.

> "The most modern English versions are [not] convincing on the level of language. . . . I find it means I am incapable of taking seriously anything that they say." —Peter Levi

Someone recalls the family reading of the King James Bible every morning this way: "Somewhere, as my father read, I became excitedly aware of . . . the beauty and glory of the words; of the images they evoke and the thoughts they can enkindle."[5] By contrast, an English Bible pitched at a junior high level is received as just that—a junior high book.

## The Beauty of Holiness

Writers on spiritual experience speak of "the numinous," by which they mean the holy and transcendent. It is a quality that belongs to God preeminently. The Bible is a book about God and the worship of God. It should possess a numinous quality—the beauty of holiness, the King James Bible called it.

Translations in the King James tradition retain the numinous quality of the original Bible. We experience it at the moment when Jesus calmed the tempest on the Sea of Galilee (Matt. 8:26). That is, we experience it in translations that retain the evocative statement that "there was a great calm" (NKJV, ESV, GNB, NLT [2004]). But there are also translations that manage to subvert and finally kill the supernatural wonder of the moment: "it was completely calm" (NIV); "everything was calm" (CEV); "a dead calm" (REB); "suddenly all was calm" (NLT); "then the wind stopped blowing" (NLV); "the sea became smooth as glass" (MESSAGE). In these latter renderings the moment of miracle has

170

been replaced by a commonplace moment on the lake where we vacation.

---

- "There are . . . many things that modern readers expect of a Bible besides clarity. One is majesty." —Stanley Edgar Hyman
- "Modern English is lacking in eloquence, in its root sense of speaking out, and its acquired meaning of speaking out from the heart." —Henry Seidel Canby
- " When I first read Romans 8 in the ESV, I knew that this was the Romans 8 of my heart." —Sinclair Ferguson

---

Solomon's prayer at the dedication of the Temple is one of the inspired and inspiring utterances in the Bible. Of course, that verdict depends somewhat on the translation from which we read the prayer. Here is a translation that retains the quality of transcendence in Solomon's address to God:

> But will God indeed dwell with man on the earth? Behold, heaven and the highest heaven cannot contain you, how much less this house that I have built! (2 Chron. 6:18, ESV; NKJV, NIV, NASB nearly identical)

Colloquializing translations manage to drain at least some of the numinous quality of Solomon's exalted words and phrases: "why, even the highest heavens cannot contain you" (NLT); "there's not enough room in all of heaven for you, LORD God" (CEV); "not even all of heaven is large enough to hold you" (GNB); "can it be that God will actually move into our neighborhood? Why, the cosmos itself isn't large enough to give you breathing room" (MESSAGE).

From my childhood, my imagination has been fired by the numinous image of "ivory palaces" (Ps. 45:8, KJV, NKJV, NASB, ESV). Influenced, no doubt, by a hymn that uses the image, I intuitively assimilated the image as a picture of a transcendent and celestial place (heaven). If I had been raised on modern translations, my imagination may not have soared to a higher plane than that of a nicely decorated suburban house: "palaces paneled with ivory" (REB); "palaces decorated with ivory" (GNB, NLT); "palaces adorned with ivory" (NIV).

## Chapter Summary

The church today needs an authoritative Word of God in the form of a Bible possessing stature and eliciting reverence. Several things conspire against our finding such a Bible. The very proliferation of translations is part of the problem. When the English-speaking world had only the King James Bible, that was what the culture meant by the concept of "the Bible." That was a great advantage to the church and to individuals, and the fact that we cannot turn back the clock should not lead us to sweep the problem of multiple translations under the carpet.

While we cannot return to an idealized past in regard to English Bible translation, we can choose between the better and the less good in regard to available translations. I propose that we are in a far stronger position with the consensus represented by essentially literal translations as opposed to the splintered scene represented by dynamic equivalent translations. The latter are often all over the board in the range with which they translate a given verse.

Additionally, some translations preserve the commanding dignity of the King James tradition, and in the passages that require it a quality of the numinous. Other modern translations often sacrifice those qualities in favor of the colloquial and common.

# 16

# TEACHING AND PREACHING

# FROM THE BIBLE

I WILL HAZARD THE GUESS that when a church board sits down to formulate what it wants in regard to preaching, the question of which Bible translation should be used is not even "on the table" as a consideration. Questions of homiletic style, the personality of the preacher, and the type of sermon seem a great deal more important than the choice of an English Bible.

The same thing is true of a Christian education board as it decides on a teaching curriculum for a church. Other issues seem a great deal more important than the question of Bible translation philosophy and practice. And when has a small group Bible study ever raised the issue of different versions of the Bible as the members laid their plans for the upcoming year?

My contention in this chapter is that the nature of preaching and Bible study is hugely influenced by the English translation that is used. In fact, certain aspects of preaching and teaching from the Bible are largely eliminated as possibilities if preachers, teachers, and Bible study members cast their lot with a dynamic equivalent translation.

## How Dynamic Equivalent Translations Pose Problems

The best way to begin thinking through the issues addressed in this chapter is by means of a series of anecdotes and vignettes that highlight what can happen with preaching and teaching when a Bible translation does not reliably give us the corresponding English words for what the authors of the Bible actually wrote. Of course, dynamic equivalent translations do not *always* let us down.

Nonetheless, the very philosophy of translation that underlies dynamic equivalent translations makes it permanently *possible* that these translations will produce the problems that I am about to outline. Furthermore, we never know *when* a dynamic equivalent translation gives us the "real thing" and when it gives us a substitute or an added overlay of editorial commentary. It is the "not knowing" that is a major part of the problem.

### The Problem of the Imaginary Bible

I recall sitting in a Sunday school class in which inductive Bible analysis formed the basis of the class. One day the text being studied included Ephesians 6:3. Essentially literal translations agree on the following rendition: "that it may go well with you and that you may live long in the land" (ESV; NKJV and NASB similar). The NIV nudges the clause "may live long" in the direction of contemporary American usage with its rendition "*enjoy long life* on the earth" (italics show the bit of contemporizing that the translators did).

The change is so small that it might seem inconsequential. But words *always* have consequences, which is the underlying theme of my entire argument. A class member seized upon the word *enjoy* and offered the interpretation that the promise of Ephesians 6:3 is not simply that a person will live long but that he or she will *enjoy* life. The colloquial "enjoy long life," offered as a more contemporaneous version of "live long," in fact introduced what I call the syndrome of the imaginary Bible—a formulation that has no basis in the original biblical text. The word *enjoy* in the English translation of Ephesians 6:3 misled the class member into making something of nothing.

It could not be otherwise with translations that substitute something for the original text. People who take the Bible seriously assume that an English translation reproduces in English what the original authors wrote. Dynamic equivalent translators do not credit Bible readers with operating on the same premise that they bring to every other book they take up, namely, that the publisher has delivered what the author wrote. Biblical preaching, teaching, and study ideally look closely at the text that people hold in their hands. By virtue of the changes that dynamic equivalent translators feel free to introduce into the text, Bible readers are consistently subject to dealing with data that is not even in the biblical text.

> "If a preacher takes his Bible into the pulpit or is preparing in his study for a sermon, and he finds that over and over again paraphrase has happened so the actual words are not there, he has two choices. He can either correct the version by telling the people, 'I'm sorry, the exact words aren't here, what it really says is this,' in which case he ruins the confidence of the people; or preaching begins to become less specific, less textually rooted and more general, broad sweeping, and I would say boring, because the points cannot be rooted with accuracy and firmness in the words of the text." —John Piper

Here is another example: a Bible study leader stands in front of a youth group with the latest edition of the New Living Translation before him. He reads the second part of James 1:18 thus: "And we, out of all creation, became his prized possession." After explicating the nuances of "prized possession," the speaker buttresses his exegesis by quoting another version that he has commended to his teenagers: ". . . showing us off as the crown of all his creatures" (MESSAGE). This yields further exploration of the exciting images of "showing off" and "crown."

The problem is that the images of prized possession and showing off a crown are not in the original. They are an

175

imaginary text. The original actually says "that we should be a kind of firstfruits of his creatures" (ESV; NASB and NKJV similar).

What I am saying is that even when the Bible has not actually disappeared from the pulpit and small group, it can still be in crisis in our churches. If preaching and teaching are consistently based on something that is not even in the original text, they mislead the public by unfolding meanings that are absent from the Bible.

I offer the following anecdote as a crowning proof for what I have said. An expert in the Greek New Testament obtained permission to produce an interlinear English-Greek New Testament based on a dynamic equivalent English translation. A person high in the publishing house involved expressed surprise that an interlinear translation had been allowed because it would show at once how many words in the dynamic equivalent translation are not present in the original text.

### *"What the Original Says Is . . . :" The Problem of Needing to Correct a Translation from the Pulpit or Lectern*

How often have you listened to a sermon in which the preacher evoked the formula, "What this verse says in the original is . . ."? Those who attend churches where topical preaching reigns hear it rarely, but that is a whole different problem. In churches where expository preaching is the norm, the formula is common, with its frequency depending on the translation that the preacher uses. A translation that regularly needs correcting by a preacher or Bible teacher is a translation with a problem.

It is the preacher's and teacher's task to explain a biblical text but not to correct it. This is where dynamic equivalent translations often let us down, and correspondingly where essentially literal translations show their worth. Except on those rare occasions where a completely literal translation would make no sense and where therefore even an essentially literal translation has changed the original, an expositor using a literal translation does not need to explain what the original "really says."

When Philip Ryken preached through the book of Galatians, he did so in an era when Tenth Presbyterian Church in Philadelphia had the NIV in the pews. Ryken's sermons accordingly had the usual quota of "what the original actually says" formulas in it. By the time Ryken revised his sermons for publication as a commentary, he had moved to an essentially literal translation. He found that he was able to remove virtually all of the caveats that his sermons had carried regarding "what the text actually says."

## The Problem of the Short-circuited Bible

The syndrome of the short-circuited Bible is as common as the problem of the imaginary Bible noted above. The short-circuited Bible is a translation in which the translators have removed the fullness of the original text and replaced it with a translation in which exegetical possibilities have been taken away. Usually this is done in the name of removing ambiguity or lack of clarity.

I remember hearing a sermon based on Psalm 24. The preacher preached an expository sermon based on the Bible in the pew—the NIV. Three times he evoked the formula, "Now, what the original actually says is . . ." I was later informed that if he had used an essentially literal translation, he would not have used the formula at all. One of the verses that my pastor corrected was verse 10, which in the NIV reads:

> Who is he, this King of glory?
> The LORD Almighty—
> he is the King of glory.

But the original text does not say "the Lord Almighty." It says "the Lord of hosts." As mentioned previously, the preface to the NIV singles out this phrase as one that has "little meaning" for modern readers. By removing the phrase "the Lord of hosts" from view, the translators removed the possibility of seeing legitimate meanings in it: the armies or citizens of heaven, for example—created beings of the spiritual realm who are under God's command. Furthermore, some commentators (including my pastor) see an eschatological

177

level of meaning in the verse—a reference to the redeemed saints in the presence of God in heaven. All of these meanings are short-circuited by the translation "Lord Almighty."

## The Credibility Gap

Jack Collins, professor of Old Testament at Covenant Seminary, pursued Hebrew lexicography (the study of word meanings) in his PhD program.[1] Upon leaving graduate school, Collins entered the ministry. Having been influenced in graduate school by dynamic equivalence as a translation practice, and desiring that his parishioners in a church plant understand the Bible, Dr. Collins used a dynamic equivalent translation for preaching and teaching.

But a problem of credibility surfaced. Because Collins is an expert in the original text of the Bible, it naturally matters to him that his preaching and teaching convey what the biblical authors actually wrote. When the translation that he was using did not deliver what the authors wrote, he found himself saying to his parishioners, "Now what the text actually says is . . ." or, "A more literal translation of the original would be . . ." This troubled Collins because (in his own words) "I sensed that sooner or later the people would neither trust their translation nor read it to listen to God's voice."[2] To make matters worse, Collins "didn't know how to be true to [his] conscience," meaning that the dominance of dynamic equivalent translations seemed to remove the very possibility of using a more literal translation, even though such a translation would be closer to what the Bible actually says.

> "An essentially literal translation of the Bible is the expositor's best friend. Its goal is the same as the expositors—to communicate clearly the meaning of what God has said in His word. Anything else threatens to obscure the text's meaning and lessen its impact on the hearer." —Garnett Reid

This, then, is another problem that dynamic equivalent translations pose for preaching, teaching, and Bible study. We can accurately call it the credibility gap. For preachers, teachers, and laypeople who have the resources to discover that dynamic equivalent translations often deliver something different from the biblical text, the Bible becomes suspect as a source of truth. If we can't trust the accuracy of our translation, we have no motivation for resorting to the Bible.

This leads me to observe that the dynamic equivalent enterprise requires a naïve reader. By that I mean that a given dynamic equivalent translation "works" for a given reader as long as the reader sticks with the dynamic equivalent translation that he or she is reading. If readers move beyond that single translation to essentially literal translations, and then to other dynamic equivalent translations, troubling divergences regularly (not always, of course) appear. The inevitable result for a thinking person is that the translation under consideration comes to lack credibility.

### Summary: How Dynamic Equivalent Translations Cause Problems

The problems that I have discussed are not simply occasional occurrences with dynamic equivalent Bibles but regular and even continuous occurrences. The issues are not small but major. The syndromes of the imaginary Bible, the translation that needs to be corrected, and the impoverished Bible strike at the heart of expository Bible preaching and inductive Bible study.

### Solutions

There is no need to belabor the ways in which an essentially literal translation helps to solve the problems that I have outlined above. The case is self-evident.

### The Real Text, Not Needing Correction

To begin, an essentially literal translation does not deliver an imaginary Bible—an English text that intersperses substitutions and additions to the original text. An essentially literal translation does not raise false issues by saying, "I came so close to the edge of the cliff" (Ps. 73:2, NLT), when the original says nothing about a cliff. Nor will it say that "God has given us a mighty Savior" (Luke 1:69, multiple dynamic equivalent translations) when the text actually says that he "has raised up a horn of salvation for us" (literal translations).

My subject in this chapter is preaching and teaching from the Bible. It is impossible to overstate the confidence that an essentially literal translation gives to a preacher, teacher, and student of the Bible. With an essentially literal translation, we do not need to keep looking back over our shoulder, wondering what mistake we might have just made in telling our charges or ourselves that the Bible says something that it does not say.

> "In writing and teaching Bible studies, I have found an essentially literal translation to be an irreplaceable and treasured guide. In light of the goal of understanding the Word that God inspired, how utterly crucial it is to have as direct access to the original words as possible. . . . What a huge help to be able to follow the logic and beauty of a passage in English translation with a high level of confidence." —Kathleen B. Nielson

Along with this confidence, we are largely delivered from the need to announce what the original "really says." What an essentially literal English translation says is what the original says, only in a different language. The problem of the credibility gap—the loss of confidence in the Bible because it often says what the original does not—is largely eliminated.

## The Fullness of the Original Text

Equal confidence comes to the preacher, teacher, or Bible student from knowing that the original text has not been short-circuited by a translation. The goal for preaching or teaching from the Bible is to present the fullness of what the original authors wrote. A translation that doles out only part of what is in the Bible is a deficient translation for biblical preaching, teaching, and study.

Of course a short-circuited Bible does not seem like a problem until one starts comparing a given dynamic equivalent translation with other translations. In the Contemporary English Version, Psalm 37:2 is a curt two-sentence unit: "They will soon disappear / like grass without rain." That is winsome in its succinctness—until we learn that half of the original verse has been omitted: "For they will soon fade like the grass / and wither like the green herb" (ESV). As for the addition of the image "without rain" in the CEV, that is just another head-scratcher that leaves a reader or audience confused.

Close reading of the text is the very essence of expository preaching and inductive Bible teaching/study. Those activities cannot exist with only a loose or vague grasp of the gist of a Bible passage. Psalm 91:1 asserts a metaphor to describe the person who trusts in God: "He who dwells in the shelter of the Most High" (ESV, NASB). There are plenty of meanings to unpack in the metaphor of dwelling in a residence—meanings like protection, relationship, proximity to others, the permanence of the situation, reliability, provision of needs, and virtually any additional association that we bring to the experience of living in a home. The following version of the statement is emaciated and inadequate for preaching and teaching: "Whoever goes to the Lord for safety" (GNB).

### Summary: Solutions

Dynamic equivalent translations have gone a long way toward removing the incentive for expository preaching, inductive Bible teaching, and careful study of the Bible. Such translations are a confusing mixture of what the biblical authors wrote, plus interpretive commentary, plus substitutions for what the original text says, that it quickly becomes hopeless to think that we can conduct a close reading of the biblical text. The problems are simply insurmountable, even if we have good intentions in the matter. The only antidote to the problem is an essentially literal translation.[3]

# Appendix A

## STATEMENTS FROM PREACHERS

## AND BIBLE STUDY EXPERTS

THE STATEMENTS in this appendix have been excerpted from personal correspondence.

"In expositional preaching, the goal is for the Word of God to deliver through the preacher a message about God, the Gospel, grace and godliness. In order to do this, the Word of God has to set the agenda of the sermon, and to fill and shape its content. The preacher's communication of the truth of the text is going to be dramatically aided by an essentially literal translation, because it will help him show his congregation the flow of argument and even the idiom of the original before he goes on to explain and apply it in terms of today's language, culture and idiom. An essentially literal translation will enhance the congregation's recognition that the pastor's exposition is derived from God's own word. Dynamic equivalency translations, however helpful they may be in many aspects, can rob a congregation of confidence that what the minister is preaching is actually anchored in the text. Essentially literal translations assist and enhance a congregation's ability to see that the truth of the sermon is rooted in and derived from the text."—J. Ligon Duncan III, senior pastor, First Presbyterian Church, Jackson, Mississippi

"I discovered the value of using a literal translation in small group Bible studies through trial and error. When I first began leading studies I thought the generous thing was to encourage people to use their favorite translation. I soon discovered that many paraphrases are a real discussion stopper. The translators often resolve any ambiguity found in the original text, so there was nothing left to discuss. Also, these paraphrases tend to move away from the concrete imagery of the original, and that tends to push the study to be more abstract than is helpful."—James Wilhoit, author, *Effective Bible Teaching*

"Teaching and preaching the Bible are enhanced by an essentially literal translation because such translations attempt to maintain word concordance within given books—so that the same root word in the original is generally translated by the same English word. This is quite helpful, for example, in preaching or teaching through the Book of Romans when the righteous/righteousness word group is regularly translated with the same words. Similarly, literal translations generally preserve the original metaphors, whereas paraphrastic translations do not. Along with this, preaching or teaching from an essentially literal translation requires less time-consuming explanation, such as, 'This morning's text reads . . . , but the word literally means. . . .' The absence of constant correction promotes people's confidence in the written word of God."—R. Kent Hughes, "senior statesman" among expository Bible preachers

"In any biblical exposition, the preacher's task is to present the words of Scripture to the congregation in such a way that, by the work of God's Spirit, they understand the importance and significance of what God says. Very often small details in the text help us to appreciate the profound significance of what is written. Too often these small details are the very things that are lost in the less literal translations. Therefore for the purposes of expository preaching the more literal translation is very much to be preferred."—John W. Woodhouse, principal, Moore College

"Essentially literal translations preserve the metaphors of the original text. The importance of this was fresh in my mind because I had been using a new dynamic equivalent translation with my children with the book of Proverbs for morning devotions over breakfast. I eventually abandoned that translation entirely because it was so much harder to understand when a proverb was abstracted from the original metaphors. An additional reason I wanted a more literal translation is that if over time I needed continually to explain what the Bible 'really says,' I ran the risk of undermining people's confidence in the Bible they were reading. I deemed it preferable to have a more literal translation that did not require some of the explanations that a dynamic equivalent translation requires."—Philip Graham Ryken, senior minister, Tenth Presbyterian Church, Philadelphia, on why he and the church moved to an essentially literal translation

"An essentially literal translation is a requirement for expository preaching for two paradoxical reasons: fidelity and freedom. Fidelity, because the whole purpose of expository preaching is to present the plain meaning of God's word with maximal faithfulness to the original text of Scripture; and the whole purpose of essentially literal translations is to be as faithful to the original as possible. Freedom, because the expository preacher, who himself wants to wrestle with the precise wording of the original text of Scripture, needs a translation that, when it comes to preaching, doesn't hem him in by already making many of his exegetical decisions for him. Instead, the expositor, having followed the text where it leads, needs a translation that allows him freedom to set forth that same text in as direct and transparent a way as possible."—Todd Wilson, senior pastor, Calvary Memorial Church, Oak Park, Illinois

"Don't interpret for me. Let me do this and let my people decide if I can prove it to them. Don't decide for me. I am going

185

to exposit this to my people. I am accountable to explain the word of God to them. You are not accountable to explain it. You are accountable to give it to me so that I can determine what it means. Don't give me a commentary. Give me a version."—John Piper, pastor for preaching and vision, Bethlehem Baptist Church, Minneapolis, in an imaginary declaration to dynamic equivalent translators.

"I cannot teach theology or ethics from a dynamic equivalent Bible. I tried the NIV for one semester, and I gave it up after a few weeks. Time and again I would try to use a verse to make a point and find that the specific detail I was looking for, a detail of wording that I knew was there in the original Hebrew or Greek, was missing from the verse in the NIV. Nor can I preach from a dynamic equivalent translation. I would end up explaining in verse after verse that the words on the page are not really what the Bible says, and the whole experience would be confusing and would lead people to distrust the Bible in English. Nor can I teach an adult Bible class at my church using a dynamic equivalence translation. I would never know what words to trust or what words have been left out. Nor can I lead our home fellowship group using a dynamic equivalent translation. Nor would I want to memorize passages from a dynamic equivalent translation. I would be fixing in my brain verses that were partly God's words and partly some added ideas, and I would be leaving out of my brain some words that belonged to those verses as God inspired them but were simply missing from the dynamic equivalence translation. But I could readily use *any* essentially literal translation to teach, study, preach from, and memorize."—Wayne Grudem, research professor of Bible and theology, Phoenix Seminary

## Summary

The following themes emerge from the foregoing testimonials about the need for an essentially literal Bible translation for purposes of preaching, teaching, and study.

- The confidence that comes from knowing that the translation puts us in touch with what the biblical authors actually wrote, without needing to worry about what a translation has omitted from the original text.

- The way in which an essentially literal translation preserves our ability to extract the full range of meanings from the biblical text, free from various types of reductionism that dynamic equivalent translators perform on the biblical text.

- The relief that comes from not needing to correct a translation with an announcement of "what the original text really says," along with the reduced respect for the Bible that accompanies that syndrome.

# Appendix B

# TEN REASONS YOU CAN TRUST
# AN ESSENTIALLY LITERAL BIBLE
# TRANSLATION

THE FOLLOWING MATERIAL is adapted from Leland Ryken's booklet *Choosing a Bible* (Wheaton, IL: Crossway Books, 2005).

You can trust an essentially literal translation of the Bible for the following ten reasons.

## 1) Transparency to the Original

*Except where a completely literal translation would have been unintelligible to an English reader, an essentially literal translation is transparent to the original text.* An essentially literal translation resists inserting an intermediary interpretive process between the reader and the original text. When on extremely rare occasions an essentially literal translation contains something other than

189

an expression of the actual words used by a biblical author, it normally contains as well an accompanying note that gives the literal rendering.

I myself can conceive of no other reason for translation than that it brings a reader as close to the original text as the process of translation allows. Why else would I read a translation of a text? It is important to note that this is a different kind of transparency than dynamic equivalent translators claim, namely, a translation that is immediately transparent to the contemporary English reader.

## 2) Keeping to the Essential Task of Translation

*You can trust an essentially literal translation to keep to the essential task of translation, namely, translation.* This is a way of saying that an essentially literal translation is not the product of a translation committee's going beyond translation to the additional tasks of an editor and exegete, either substituting material in the place of what the original says or adding interpretive commentary to the biblical text.

## 3) Preserving the Full Interpretive Potential of the Original

*You can trust an essentially literal translation to preserve the full interpretive potential of the original text.* An essentially literal translation resists the following common forms of reductionism that afflict dynamic equivalent translations:

- simplifying the original text to a lowest common denominator of contemporary readers;
- choosing just one of the potential meanings of a passage and putting only that in front of the reader;
- making preemptive interpretive strikes so as to prevent the reader from making interpretive decisions for himself or herself;
- eliminating technical or difficult theological vocabulary and substituting nontechnical vocabulary;
- interpreting figurative language right in the translation;

190

- assuming that modern readers are inferior to both the original audience of the Bible and readers of the English Bible through the centuries;
- reducing the level of vocabulary;
- diminishing the literary beauty and exaltation of the Bible;
- paring down the affective power of the Bible;
- reducing the stylistic variety of the original text to a monotone arrived at by slanting the translation toward a target audience with allegedly low linguistic and cognitive abilities.

Stated positively, you can trust an essentially literal translation to do the following things as a way of preserving the full richness and exegetical potential of the Bible. An essentially literal translation will preserve:

- language as beautiful and sophisticated as the original itself possesses;
- as many levels of meaning as the original contains;
- poetry in its original, literal expression;
- the stylistic range of the original;
- theological terminology as complex as the original contains.

The goal of an essentially literal translation is fullness. The effect of dynamic equivalent translations has been diminishment—diminishment in the form of reduced expectations of Bible readers, reduced respect for biblical authors, impoverishment of language, emaciated theology, a one-dimensional Bible in regard to legitimate multiple meanings, and lowered literary standards.

## 4) Not Mixing Commentary with Translation

*You can trust an essentially literal translation not to mislead you.* We normally operate on the premise that the book that a publisher or translator puts into our hands is what the original author actually wrote. Within the necessary changes that all translation requires, an essentially literal translation does not betray that trust. It keeps to an absolute minimum the intermingling of interpretive commentary with translation. An essentially literal translation operates on the premise that a translator is a steward of what someone else has written, not an editor and exegete who needs to help or correct what someone else has written.

## 5) Preserving Theological Precision

*You can trust an essentially literal translation to preserve theological precision.* We cannot build an adequate theology without an adequate theological vocabulary. A theological concept of justification can be built on the statement (Rom. 3:24) that we "are justified by his grace as a gift" (ESV) but not on such dynamic equivalent paraphrases as we "are put right with [God]" [GNB] or "God in his gracious kindness declares us not guilty" (NLT) or "God treats us much better than we deserve" (CEV).

## 6) Not Needing to Correct the Translation in Preaching and Teaching

*You can trust an essentially literal translation to prevent an expository preacher or teacher from needing to correct the biblical text.* One of the reasons for the decline in expository preaching and inductive Bible study is that in the wake of the dynamic equivalent revolution English translations of the Bible consistently need to be corrected from the pulpit and in the small-group Bible study. It is impossible to conduct a close reading of an unreliable text. You can trust an essentially literal translation largely to eliminate the need to resort to the formula "now what the original actually says is . . ."

## 7) Preserving What the Biblical Writers Actually Wrote

*You can trust an essentially literal translation not to resolve all interpretive difficulties in the direction of what a given translation committee decides to parcel out to its readers.* You can expect a literal translation to pass on interpretive difficulties to the reader. Is this a virtue? It is. The goal is to know what the original authors said. If they passed difficulties on to *their* readers, translators need to do the same.

## 8) Preserving the Literary Qualities of the Bible

*If your essentially literal translation is the RSV, the ESV, or the NKJV—in other words, if your essentially literal translation rides the literary coattails of the matchless KJV—you can trust it to preserve the literary qualities of the Bible that the KJV gave to the English-speaking world for nearly four centuries.* The Bible in its original is a very literary book. We need to understand that if we believe that the Holy Spirit inspired the authors of the Bible, it was ultimately the Holy Spirit who gave us a literary Bible replete with poetry, for example. It was the Holy Spirit who gave us figurative language, and an essentially literal translation preserves that figurative language.

## 9) Preserving the Dignity and Beauty of the Bible

*You can trust some essentially literal translations to preserve the exaltation, dignity, and beauty of the Bible.* You can expect to read, "Behold, I stand at the door and knock" (Rev. 3:20, KJV, NASB, ESV), not such things as this: "Here I am! I stand at the door and knock" (NIV, TNIV), or, "Here I stand knocking at the door" (REB), or, "Listen! I am standing and knocking at your door" (CEV). In an essentially literal translation you will find the awe-inspiring lead-in, "Truly, truly, I say to you" (ESV), not a translation that has scaled the voltage down to "I tell you the truth" (NIV) or "I tell you for certain" (CEV) or "I assure you" (NLT). In a translation in the King James tradition, the beloved in the Song of Solomon will be brought "to the banqueting house" (Song 2:4, ESV), not to a "special large room for eating" (NLV), and the beloved will attest that "his banner over me was love" (Song 2:4, ESV), not that "it's obvious how much he loves me" (NLT, 2004).

## 10) Consistency with the Doctrine of Inspiration

*You can trust an essentially literal translation to adhere to the implications of the doctrine of plenary or verbal inspiration.* Such a translation believes that the very words of the Bible are inspired and therefore inviolable. Another way of saying this is that an essentially literal translation will not lead you unwittingly to violate the very principle of verbal inspiration that you endorse. Throughout the Bible, Scripture is referred to as the Word of God, not the thought(s) of God. Jesus himself said that "*the words* that I have spoken to you are spirit and life" (John 6:63, ESV).

## Conclusion

English Bible translation stands at a watershed moment. For half a century, dynamic equivalence has been the guiding translation philosophy behind most new translations. Each successive wave of these translations has tended to be increasingly bold in departing from the words of the original text. Stated another way, we can trace an arc of increasingly aggressive changing, adding to, and subtracting from the words that the biblical authors wrote.

The issues that are at stake in the current debate about Bible translation are immense. Boiled down to its essence, at stake is whether English Bible readers will have the Word of God or a mixture of God's Word with human commentary and interpretation.

# NOTES

## Preface

1. *The Word of God in English: Criteria for Excellence in Bible Translation* (Wheaton, IL: Crossway, 2002).

## Chapter 1: Understanding English Bible Translation

1. *The Word of God in English: Criteria for Excellence in Bible Translation* (Wheaton, IL: Crossway, 2002), 187–97.

2. D. A. Carson, "The Limits of Functional Equivalence in Bible Translation—and Other Limits, Too," in *The Challenge of Bible Translation*, ed. Glen G. Scorgie, et al. (Grand Rapids, MI: Zondervan, 2003), 66.

## Chapter 2: Questions and Answers about English Bible Translation

1. Mark Strauss, review of *The Word of God in English*, by Leland Ryken, *Journal of the Evangelical Theological Society* 46 (2003): 739.

2. Gordon D. Fee and Mark L. Strauss, *How to Choose a Translation for All Its [sic] Worth* (Grand Rapids, MI: Zondervan, 2007), 32.

3. Strauss, *Journal of the Evangelical Theological Society*, 739.

4. Raymond C. Van Leeuwen, "We Really Do Need Another Bible Translation," *Christianity Today*, October 22, 2001, 30.

5. Jan de Waard and Eugene A. Nida, *From One Language to Another: Functional Equivalence in Bible Translating* (Nashville: Thomas Nelson, 1986), 39. Nida made this statement specifically in regard to resolving ambiguities in the original, but the argument is applied generally by dynamic equivalent translators.

## Chapter 3: Laying the Foundation

1. Alec Gilmore, *A Dictionary of the English Bible and Its Origins* (Sheffield, UK: Sheffield Academic Press, 2000), 186.

2. David Daniell, *The Bible in English: Its History and Influence* (New Haven, CT: Yale University Press, 2003), 158, 248–54.

3. All quotations from Tyndale's New Testament are taken from *Tyndale's New Testament*, ed. David Daniell (New Haven, CT: Yale University Press, 1989).

4. Benson Bobrick, *Wide as the Waters: The Story of English Bible and the Revolution It Inspired* (New York: Penguin, 2001), 105.

5. I have borrowed the formula "biblical culture" from Christopher Hill, *The English Bible and the Seventeenth-Century Revolution* (London: Penguin, 1993), 3.

6. John Strype, as quoted in John Brown, *The History of the English Bible* (Cambridge: Cambridge University Press, 1911), 67.

7. Even David Daniell, who exaggerates the plainness of Tyndale's style, acknowledges that Tyndale's style was "a notch above ordinary speech" (158). It is more accurate to say that it was several notches above ordinary speech.

8. Hill, *The English Bible*, 15.

9. J. W. Martin, *Religious Radicals in Tudor England* (London: Hambledon Press, 1989).

10. Hill, *The English Bible*, 39.

11. Daniell, *The Bible in English*, 266.

12. Hill, *The English Bible*, 11; Daniell, *The Bible in English*, 271.

## Chapter 4: Building on the Foundation

1. Good treatments can be found in the following sources: Benson Bobrick, *Wide as the Waters: The Story of the English Bible and the Revolution It Inspired* (New York: Penguin, 2002); David Daniell, *The Bible in English: Its History and Influence* (New Haven: Yale University Press, 2003); Alister McGrath, *In the Beginning: The Story of King James Bible and How It Changed a Nation, a Language, and a Culture* (New York: Anchor Books, 2002); Adam Nicolson, *God's Secretaries: The Making of the King James Bible* (New York: HarperCollins, 2003).

2. Bobrick, *Wide as the Waters*, 258.

3. From the fourteenth rule (of fifteen) governing the translation, as quoted in McGrath, *In the Beginning*, 175.

4. Ibid., 177–78.

5. Ibid., 250.

6. Ibid., 254.

7. Daniell, *The Bible in English*, 429.

8. Craig R. Thompson, *The Bible in English, 1525–1611* (Ithaca, NY: Cornell University Press, 1958), 27.

9. Examples include Bobrick, *Wide as the Waters*, 254; McGrath, *In the Beginning*, 262.

10. Bobrick, *Wide as the Waters*, 262.

11. McGrath, *In the Beginning*, 252.

12. Geddes MacGregor, *A Literary History of the Bible from the Middle Ages to the Present Day* (Nashville: Abingdon, 1968), 206.

13. Throughout the preface to the RSV, reference is made to the KJV, not to the American Standard Version.

## Chapter 5: Building on Another Foundation

1. Eugene A. Nida, *Good News for Everyone: How to Use the Good News Bible* (Waco, TX: Word, 1977), 10.
2. Eugene A. Nida, "Meaning-full Translations," *Christianity Today*, October 7, 2002, 48.
3. Ibid., 46.
4. Ibid., 49.
5. John Beekman and John Callow, *Translating the Word of God* (Grand Rapids, MI: Zondervan, 1974), 25.
6. Mark L. Strauss, "Form, Function, and the 'Literal Meaning' Fallacy in Bible Translation," address at the 2003 annual meeting of the Evangelical Theological Society, accessed online.
7. Ibid.

## Chapter 6: Divergent Goals for Bible Translation

1. Billy Graham, preface to *The Living Letters* (Wheaton, IL: Tyndale, 1967).
2. Stephen Prickett, *Words and the Word: Language, Poetics and Biblical Interpretation* (Cambridge: Cambridge University Press, 1986), 4.
3. Y. C. Whang, "To Whom Is a Translator Responsible—Reader or Author?" in *Translating the Bible: Problems and Prospects*, ed. Stanley E. Porter and Richard S. Hess (Sheffield, UK: Sheffield Academic Press, 1999), 46–62.
4. Eugene A. Nida and Charles R. Taber, *The Theory and Practice of Translation* (Leiden: E. J. Brill, 1969), 31.
5. Nida and Taber, *Theory and Practice*, 32.
6. John MacArthur, endorsement of Leland Ryken, *The Word of God in English* (Wheaton, IL: Crossway, 2002).
7. Eugene A. Nida, "Meaning-full Translations," *Christianity Today*, October 7, 2002, 46.
8. Gordon D. Fee and Mark L. Strauss, *How to Choose a Translation for All Its [sic] Worth* (Grand Rapids, MI: Zondervan, 2007), 27.
9. Nida, "Meaning-full Translations," 48.
10. C. John Collins, appendix to Leland Ryken, *The Word of God in English* (Wheaton, IL: Crossway, 2002), 295.
11. Eugene H. Glassman, *The Translation Debate: What Makes a Bible Translation Good?* (Downers Grove, IL: InterVarsity, 1981), 47.

## Chapter 7: Divergent Views of the Bible

1. Billy Graham, preface to *The Living Letters* (Wheaton, IL: Tyndale, 1967).
2. Gordon D. Fee and Mark L. Strauss, *How to Choose a Translation for All Its [sic] Worth* (Grand Rapids, MI: Zondervan, 2007), 29.
3. Ibid., 33.
4. Raymond C. Van Leeuwen, "We Really Do Need Another Bible Translation," *Christianity Today*, October 22, 2001, 33.
5. The statement was made by a member of the Bible Society that produced the Good News Bible, in a letter to the editor of *Theology*, May 1978, quoted in Stephen Prickett, *Words and the Word* (Cambridge: Cambridge University Press, 1986), 6.
6. Ibid.

## Chapter 8: Divergent Views of the Bible's Authors, Readers, and Translators

1. On many of the subjects covered in this book, I myself have the most extensive published discussion in *The Word of God in English: Criteria for Excellence in Bible Translation* (Wheaton, IL: Crossway, 2002).

2. Robert G. Bratcher, as quoted in Jack P. Lewis, *The English Bible from KJV to NIV: A History and Evaluation* (Grand Rapids, MI: Baker, 1981), 263.

3. Christopher Hill, *The English Bible and the Seventeenth-Century Revolution* (London: Penguin, 1993), 39; David Daniell, *The Bible in English: Its History and Influence* (New Haven, CT: Yale University Press, 2003), chap. 15.

4. Tony Naden "Understandest Thou What Thou Readest?" *The Bible Translator* 33 (1982): 33. For a similar sentiment, see Robert Martin, *Accuracy of Translation* (Edinburgh: Banner of Truth, 1989), 29.

5. E. V. Rieu, "Translating the Gospels: A Discussion Between Dr. E. V. Rieu and the Rev. J. B. Phillips," *The Bible Translator* 6/4 (October 1955): 154.

6. For a quick induction into this kind of thinking, it is hard to beat Eugene A. Nida's book *Good News for Everyone* (Waco, TX: Word, 1977).

7. I am getting my information about the differences between the herald and orator of Greco-Roman culture from A. Duane Litfin's essay "Swallowing Our Pride: An Essay on the Foolishness of Preaching," in *Preach the Word*, ed. Leland Ryken and Todd Wilson (Wheaton, IL: Crossway, 2007), 116–19. It is truly fascinating and revealing to read Litfin's contrast between herald and orator with essentially literal and dynamic equivalent translators in mind.

8. Ibid., 117.

## Chapter 9: Divergent Methods of Translation

1. Francis R. Steele, "Translation or Paraphrase," in *The New Testament Student and Bible Translation*, ed. John Skilton (Phillipsburg, NJ: P&R, 1978), 69.

2. Eugene A. Nida, *Good News for Everyone* (Waco, TX: Word, 1977), 14.

3. Gordon D. Fee and Mark L. Strauss, *How to Choose a Translation for All Its [sic] Worth* (Grand Rapids, MI: Zondervan, 2007), 32.

4. Dwight Macdonald, "The Bible in Modern Undress," in *Literary Style of the Old Bible and the New*, ed. D. G. Kehl (Indianapolis: Bobbs-Merrill, 1970), 40.

## Chapter 10: Divergent Styles of Translation

1. Eugene A. Nida and Charles R. Taber, *The Theory and Practice of Translation* (Leiden: E. J. Brill, 1969), 7. Nida repeats the anecdote in *Good News for Everyone* (Waco, TX: Word, 1977), 10.

2. Gordon D. Fee and Mark L. Strauss, *How to Choose a Translation for All Its [sic] Worth* (Grand Rapids, MI: Zondervan, 2007), 29.

3. Eugene H. Glassman, *The Translation Debate* (Downers Grove, IL: InterVarsity, 1981), 43.

4. Fee and Strauss, *How to Choose a Translation*, 27.

## Chapter 11: Fullness Rather Than Reductionism

1. Aristophanes, *Frogs* [405 B.C.].

2. Jan de Waard and Eugene A. Nida, *From One Language to Another: Functional Equivalence in Bible Translating* (Nashville: Thomas Nelson, 1986), 39, regard it as "unfair to the original writer and to the receptors to reproduce as ambiguities

all those passages which may be interpreted in more than one way." Eugene H. Glassman, *The Translation Debate* (Downers Grove, IL: InterVarsity, 1981), 101, asserts the translation principle, "Avoid ambiguity. We translate/paraphrase dynamically when a literal/formal translation would be *ambiguous.*"

3. Raymond C. Van Leeuwen, "We Really Do Need Another Bible Translation," *Christianity Today*, October 22, 2201, 32.

4. Alec Gilmore, *A Dictionary of the English Bible and Its Origins* (Sheffield, UK: Sheffield Academic Press, 2000), 54.

5. Quoted by Stephen Prickett, *Words and the Word: Language, Poetics and Biblical Interpretation* (Cambridge: Cambridge University Press, 1986), 6.

## Chapter 12: Transparency to the Original Text

1. Flannery O'Conner, *Mystery and Manners* (New York: Farrar, Straus and Giroux, 1963, 1969), 75; italics added.

2. Raymond C. Van Leeuwen, "On Bible Translation and Hermeneutics," in *After Pentecost: Language and Biblical Interpretation*, ed. Craig Bartholomew, et al. (Grand Rapids: MI: Zondervan, 2001), 307.

3. Eugene A. Nida, however, finds this stylistic trait of biblical writers to be "childish" (Eugene A. Nida and Charles R. Taber, *The Theory and Practice of Translation* [Leiden: E. J. Brill, 1969], 14),

4. Raymond C. Van Leeuwen, "We Really Do Need Another Bible Translation," *Christianity Today*, October 22, 2001, 30.

## Chapter 13: Preserving the Literary Qualities of the Bible

1. Artur Weiser, *The Psalms: A Commentary* (Philadelphia: Westminster, 1962), 585.

2. Anthony Howard Nichols, "Translating the Bible: A Critical Analysis of E. A. Nida's Theory of Dynamic Equivalence and Its Impact upon Recent Bible Translations," dissertation, University of Sheffield, 1996, 300.

3. Eugene A. Nida, *Good News for Everyone* (Waco, TX: Word, 1977), 9–10.

## Chapter 14: Oral Reading of the Bible

1. H. L. Mencken, *Treatise on the Gods* (New York: Knopf, 1946), 286.

2. Dwight Macdonald, "The Bible in Modern Undress," in *Literary Style of the Old Bible and the New*, ed. D. G. Kehl (Indianapolis: Bobbs-Merrill, 1970), 38.

3. F. L. Lucas, "The Greek 'Word' Was Different," in *Literary Style of the Old Bible*, 51.

4. John Livingston Lowes, "The Noblest Monument of English Prose," in *Literary Style of the Old Bible*, 15.

5. Dorothy Thompson, "The Old Bible and the New," in *Literary Style of the Old Bible*, 46.

## Chapter 15: The Need for a Translation That People Can Trust and Respect

1. Gary Burge, "The Greatest Story Never Read," *Christianity Today*, August 9, 1999, 45–49; Woodrow Kroll, *Taking Back the Good Book* (Wheaton, IL: Crossway, 2007).

2. George A. Lindbeck, "The Church's Mission to a Postmodern Culture," in *Postmodern Theology: Christian Faith in a Pluralist World* (San Francisco: Harper and Row, 1989), 45.

3. This rendition is rightly demolished by David Daniell, *The Bible in English: Its History and Influence* (New Haven, CT: Yale University Press, 2003), 758.

4. Billy Graham, preface to *The Living Letters* (Wheaton, IL: Tyndale, 1967).

5. Dorothy Thompson, "The Old Bible and the New," in *Literary Style of the Old Bible and the New*, ed. D. G. Kehl (Indianapolis: Bobbs-Merrill, 1970), 44.

### Chapter 16: Teaching and Preaching from the Bible

1. Jack Collins recounts his experience in the appendix he authored to Leland Ryken, *The Word of God in English: Criteria for Excellence in Bible Translation* (Wheaton, IL: Crossway, 2002), 296–97.

2. Ibid., 296.

3. For more statements by preachers and Bible study experts on the advantages of an essentially literal translation, see Appendix A.

# INDEX

Abdi, Cyrus, 63
Alter, Robert, 104
ambiguity, in literary writing and transla-
tion, 143–45, 200–201n2
American Standard Version, 53
Aristophanes, 122

Barfield, Owen, 115
Bible, the, 39, 62–63, 79, 107–8, 132,
138, 151, 170, 172; as an ancient
book, 81–82; as an ancient/modern
book, 79, 116–17; authors of, 89; as
a book needing correction, 85–87;
contrasting views of, 84–85; diminished respect for biblical authors,
90–91, 116; exegetical potential of,
125–27; fullness of the original text,
121–22, 128–29, 180–81; modernization of the biblical text, 80–81;
poetry of, 147–49; the quest for a
colloquial Bible, 110–11; respect
for, 167–68, 172; as a simple book,
83–84; stable and destabilized text of,
164–67; teaching from, 173. See also
Bible, the, literary qualities of; Bible,
the, readers of; dynamic equivalence;
dynamic equivalent translations,
problems concerning; translation
Bible, the, literary qualities of, 139;
importance of the Bible's literary dimension, 139–41; literary genres and

subtypes in the Bible, 139–40; multilayered discourse, 143–45; mystery
and subtlety, 145–47; and respect for
an author's literary intention, 141–43
Bible, the, readers of, 91, 175; dynamic
equivalence view of, 92–93; literal
translators' view of, 93–95
biblical illiteracy, 163–64
Bishop's Bible, 44, 49
Bobrick, Benson, 48
Brooks, Cleanth, 77
Butterworth, Charles, 51

Camus, Albert, 136
Canby, Henry Seidel, 169, 171
*Canterbury Tales* (Chaucer), 82
Carson, D. A., 18, 82
*Choosing a Bible* (L. Ryken), 189
Ciardi, John, 51
Collins, Jack, 78, 178
Contemporary English Version (CEV),
109, 180–81
correspondence, 21; verbal, 103
Coverdale, Miles, 43
Coverdale's Bible, 43, 45

Daniell, David, 41, 50, 123, 128, 136,
146; on Tyndale's style, 198n7
David, 109, 110
Duncan, J. Ligon, 183–84
dynamic, 21

201

dynamic equivalence, 19, 21–22, 24, 25–27, 29, 30–32, 57–58, 66, 99, 103, 114, 128, 133, 151, 164; approach of to idiomatic expressions, 115–16; and the "correction" of the Bible, 85–86; critique of, 145; as paraphrase, 105–6; primacy of abstraction in, 111–13; and reader subjectivity, 138; and the removal of metaphor from Bible translation, 141–43; statements from expositional preachers concerning, 183–183; and the transparency of the text, 72–74, 131; usefulness of dynamic equivalent translations, 32; and the word versus meaning debate, 75–78. See also dynamic equivalent translations, problems concerning; translators, dynamic equivalent translators

dynamic equivalent, 18

dynamic equivalent translations, problems concerning, 174; problem of correcting translation from the pulpit, 176–77; problem of the credibility gap, 178–79; problem of the imaginary Bible, 174–76; problem of the short-circuited Bible, 177–78; solutions to the problems, 179–81

Esau, 58–59
Eliot, T. S., 110, 123, 160
Elizabeth I, 44
English Standard Version (ESV), 32, 47, 54, 73, 156, 157
equivalence, 20–21; equivalent effect, 19; formal equivalence, 19; "full" equivalence, 121; functional equivalence, 19, 21, 25–27; verbal equivalence, 19. See also dynamic equivalence
Erasmus, 38
essentially literal translation. See translation, literal

Fee, Gordon, 63, 77, 107–8
Ferguson, Sinclair, 171
form, and meaning, 77–78
Frye, Northrop, 112

"gender generic" ("inclusive") language, 85–86
Geneva Bible, 43–44, 45, 48, 50, 75, 86

God, 83, 147–48, 149; as the "Lord of hosts," 136–37, 177–78
Good News Bible, 62, 71, 72, 92, 103, 112–13, 128, 153; biblical poetry style of, 59–61, 149; narrative style of, 58–59
Graham, Billy, 72, 80–81, 169
Great Bible, the, 43
Grudem, Wayne, 186

Hammond, Gerald, 104, 144
Henry VIII, 43
Herbert, George, 105
Hill, Christopher, 45
Hirsch, E. D., 142
Hodges, Zane C., 165
holiness, beauty of, 170–72
Holy Spirit, the, 148, 149
Hughes, R. Kent, 184
Hyman, Stanley Edgar, 146, 171

ideas, consequences of, 102–3
illiteracy. See biblical illiteracy
interpretation, lexical and linguistic, 23–24

Jacob, 58–59
James I, 48
Jarrett-Kerr, Martin, 123
Jesus Christ, 83, 144, 169, 169; calming of the sea by, 170–71; "hard sayings" of, 143; parables of, 84–85; as the propitiation for our sins, 128–29

King James Version (KJV), 40, 45, 47, 57, 65, 123, 136, 156, 160, 161, 172; affective power of, 167–68, 169–70; authority of, 167–68; beauty of language in, 50; flexible style of, 51; meter of, 51–52; production and translation procedures of, 47–50, 52–53; qualities of, 50–52; rhythm of, 154–55; tradition of, 53–55, 60
Krutch, Joseph Wood, 136

language: donor, 18; native, 18; receptor, 18
Latin Vulgate, 37, 38
Levi, Peter, 170
Lewis, C. S., 112, 140
linguistic conservatism, 20

linguistic theory, 27–29
Linton, Calvin, 60
literature: ambiguity in, 143–45, 200–201n2; concrete aspect of, 141; difference of from oral communication, 141; genres and subtypes of, 139–40; mystery and subtlety in, 145–47
Litfin, A. Duane, 200n7
Living Letters, The, 72, 80–81
Lowes, John Livingston, 49, 51, 112
Lucas, F. L., 110, 161

MacArthur, John, 75
Macaulay, Thomas, 51
Macdonald, Dwight, 110, 160, 169
Mallarmé, Stéphane, 77
Martin, J. W., 45
Martin, Robert, 93
Mary, Queen of Scots (Mary Stuart), 43, 45
Matthew, Thomas, 43
Matthew's Bible, 43
McGrath, Alister, 49–50, 54, 123
McLuhan, Marshall, 77
Mencken, H. L., 51, 160
Message, The, 18, 19, 86, 109, 125
metaphors/metaphoric language, 74, 85, 126; biblical, 148; removal of from dynamic equivalence translations, 141–43, 149

New American Standard Bible (NASB), 32, 53–54, 156, 157
New Century Version (NCV), 90
New English Bible (NEB), 156, 157
New International Version (NIV), 18, 31–32, 65, 90, 108–9, 148, 153, 156, 158, 168, 174, 177
New King James Version (NKJV), 32, 47, 54, 75, 121, 157
New Living Translation (NLT), 30, 71, 76, 94, 115, 148, 175
New Revised Standard Version (NRSV), 156
New Testament, 39, 70, 80, 136, 138; Greek, 38, 176
Nichols, Anthony Howard, 84, 126, 136, 144; critique of dynamic equivalence translations, 145
Nicolson, Adam, 51, 155, 167

Nida, Eugene, 20–21, 31, 60, 61, 62, 64, 76, 103, 107, 149, 197n5; on meaning in written texts, 77; on the needs of the audience versus author allegiance, 74–75; on the role of the translator, 97
Nielson, Kathleen B., 180
NIV Reconsidered, The (Radmacher and Hodges), 165

O'Connor, Flannery, 112, 132
Old Testament, 38, 42, 111, 136
oral discourse, 141

Palmer, Edwin H., 60
paraphrase: definition of, 103–4; practice of, 104–6; of Psalm 23, 105; verbal correspondence versus paraphrase, 103
patriarchalism, 85
Paul, 81, 90, 94, 169; use of metaphor by, 111 12
Peterson, Eugene, 81
Piper, John, 175, 185–86
poetry, 168; poetic rhythm, 155; poetic rhythm in Psalms 24, 48, and 104, 155–59; translation of, 100–101, 108–9, 125–27, 147–49
Prickett, Stephen, 72
"Problem of the Transparent Text, The" (Prickett), 72
prose, 101–2, 161, 168; prose narrative, 109–10
Protestantism, 44
Puritans, 48

Radmacher, Earl, 165
Rauber, D. H., 91
readability, 29
reductionism, linguistic, 121–22, 125
Reid, Garnett, 178
Religious Radicals in Tudor England (Martin), 45
Revised English Bible (REB), 157, 158, 168
Revised Standard Version (RSV), 47, 53, 54, 70, 156, 157, 198n13; style of biblical poetry in, 59–61; style of narrative in, 58–59
rhythm, 153–54; elements of, 154; importance of good rhythm, 160–61; in

the King James Version of the Bible, 154–55; poetic rhythm, 155–59; prose rhythm, 159–60
Rieu, E. V., 95
Rodgers, John. *See* Matthew, Thomas
Roman Catholicism, 38, 43, 44, 45
Ruth, character of in various Bible translations, 122–23
Ryken, Leland, 189
Ryken, Philip, 177, 185

Samuel, 124–25
Saul, 109, 123–25; Samuel's rebuke of, 124–25
Sayers, Dorothy, 112
sexual euphemisms, 114–15, 137
Simplified English Bible, 103, 128
Sittler, Joseph, 134
Skilton, John H., 82, 97
Steele, Francis R., 106
*Stranger, The* (Camus), 136
Strauss, Mark, 27, 63, 77, 107–8

Taber, Charles, 63
text(s): accuracy of, 77; preserving versus changing styles of, 113; preserving the words of the original text, 136–37; preserving the world of the original text, 133–35; stylistics involved in, 135–36; transparency and translation of original text, 20, 137–38
theological fullness, 128–29
Thompson, Craig, 155
Thompson, Dorothy, 161
Today's English Version, 107
translation, 17–18, 119, 172; colloquializing of, 141, 168, 171; communal nature of, 44–45; concepts underlying, 18–20; contrasting narrative styles in, 58–59; contrasting styles of biblical poetry in, 59–61; distinction between what a text "says" and what it "means," 27–29; distinctions between rival translation philosophies, 32–33; formal versus colloquial styles of, 107–8; genres of, 67; goal of, 64; history of, 35, 37, 42–44; as lexical and linguistic interpretation, 23–24; "new orthodoxy" of, 17; paradigm shifts in, 57–58; in the period between Tyndale and the King James

Version, 42–44; of prose, 101–2; of prose narrative, 109–10; reasons for the paradigm shift in biblical translation, 64–66; retention of theological fullness in, 128–29; shared goals of Bible translators, 70–71. *See also* dynamic equivalence; poetry, translation of; translation, differing goals of; translation, issues concerning; translation, literal; translation, new philosophies concerning
translation, differing goals of, 69, 71, 78; allegiance to author or to audience, 74–75; opposing views on transparency, 72–74; translating words versus translating meaning, 75–78
translation, issues concerning: "dynamic equivalence" and "functional equivalence" as descriptors, 25–26; "dynamic equivalence" and "functional equivalence" as objectionable concepts, 26–27, 30–32; endorsement of dynamic equivalent translation, 29; linguistic theory and the original text, 27–29; usefulness of dynamic equivalent translations, 32; view that all translation is interpretation, 23–25; words versus meaning debate, 75–78; worthiness of dynamic equivalent translations, 29
translation, literal, 19–20, 23, 27, 82, 99, 172; and the "correction" of Bible, 86–87; implied view of concerning Bible "correction," 91; need for in preaching and Bible study, 186–87; of Psalm 103 (vv. 1–5), 108; as solution to the problem of the "imaginary Bible," 179–80; statements from expositional preachers concerning, 183–186; and transparency of the text, 131–32. *See also* translation, literal, reasons for trusting
translation, literal, reasons for trusting: consistency with the doctrine of inspiration, 193–94; maintenance of the essential task of translation, 190; not having to correct translation in preaching, 192; preservation of the Bible's dignity and beauty, 193; preservation of the interpretive potential

of the original text, 190–91; preservation of the literary qualities of the Bible, 193; preservation of theological precision, 192; preservation of what biblical writers actually wrote, 192–93; separation of commentary from translation, 191–92; transparency to the original, 189–90

translation, new philosophies concerning, 61–62, 66; demotion of the words of the original text, 63–64; translating for a specific audience, 62–63

translators, 28–29, 75–76, 95; dynamic equivalent translators, 29, 31, 96–97, 101, 132, 141–43, 146–47, 149, 167, 175, 197n5; and fidelity to the original text, 99–100; implied view of literal translators, 91; literal translators' view of transparency, 132; metaphors for rival views of translators (herald/orator distinction), 97–98, 200n7

transliteration, 27

transparency, 72–74, 131–32, 137–38; concept of transparent text, 20, 72; defining the ideal of, 132–33

Tyndale, William, 37, 45, 46, 70, 94, 123; clarity of his style, 39–40, 198n7; influence of on the English language, 40, 41; legacy of, 40–42; translation principles of, 38–40; as a translator, 37–38

Van Leeuwen, Raymond, 28, 82, 101, 126, 134, 138, 148

vocabulary: concrete versus abstract, 111; effect of scaled-down vocabulary on biblical content, 122–25

Weeks, Noel K., 128

Wilhoit, James, 184

Wilson, Todd, 185

Woodhouse, John W., 185

Word of God in English, The (L. Ryken), 17, 200n1

Wieun, C. L., 169

Wycliffe Bible, 37

# PERMISSIONS